Spectacular Stars Simplified

STITCH & FLIP QUILTS WITH A LONE STAR LOOK

Shelley Cavanna

C&T PUBLISHING
Another Maker Inspired!

Copyright © 2020 by Michelle N. Cavanna

Publisher: Amy Barrett-Daffin

Creative Director: Gailen Runge

Senior Editor: Roxane Cerda

Copy Editor: Melissa Bryan

Text and Cover Design: Adrienne Smitke

Photographer: Brent Kane

Illustrator: Sandy Loi

Production Coordinator: Zinnia Heinzmann

Published by C&T Publishing, Inc., P.O. Box 1456, Lafayette, CA 94549

Attention Teachers: C&T Publishing, Inc., encourages the use of our books as texts for teaching. You can find lesson plans for many of our titles at ctpub.com or contact us at ctinfo@ctpub.com.

Library of Congress Control Number: 2023934773

Printed in the USA

10 9 8 7 6 5 4 3 2 1

SPECIAL THANKS

Photography for this book was taken at the homes of:
Bree Larson of Everett, Washington
Stephanie Sullivan of Issaquah, Washington

DEDICATION

To Rob, for your constant love and encouragement . . . and all the laughter along the way!

And to Aiden and Jamie. Always chase after your own stars!

Contents

Introduction

Like so many of my quilty friends, I've had a Lone Star quilt on my bucket list for some time, and I've had a number of Lone Star–esque patterns quietly bubbling around in the back of my brain. These quilts and designs have stayed on my quilting back burner, however, because they have a reputation for being notoriously tricky and time-consuming.

Traditionally, Lone Star quilts are assembled using a large number of diamond pieces (with loads of bias edges), which are sewn into larger diamond or triangle sections. These sections are then joined to background units or other sections with inset or Y-seams. And while plenty of quilters successfully use these traditional methods to make gorgeous quilts, these just aren't my favorite techniques to use.

So, after a great deal of experimentation, I came up with a way to use some of my favorite building blocks, like Flying Geese and Half-Log-Cabin blocks, along with some clever little stitch-and-flip diamonds to put together Lone Stars of all shapes and sizes with nary a bias edge or inset seam in sight.

I don't like to make quilts (or write patterns!) that require templates, angular cutting, or inset seams. I prefer to avoid bias edges as much as humanly possible. Because those edges are so stretchy, they require quite a bit of additional time spent wrestling them into submission or getting them to play nicely with their neighboring units. All that frustration and extra fiddling takes quite a bit of the joy out of my already limited quilting time. As a mom to two very active and rambunctious boys, I prefer to spend my precious, uninterrupted studio time at my machine, sewing . . . and getting as much pleasure out of the construction process as I get from the finished quilt!

My mission, not only as a quilt designer but also as a teacher, is to do the same for you! I love taking marvelously complex-looking quilts and breaking them down into *small, easy-to-piece, and quick-to-sew units* in shapes that you're probably already familiar with or that are quick and easy to learn if you're not. In fact, my whole business motto is *stunning quilts made simple.*

I hope you'll enjoy creating these beautiful Lone Star variations as much as I did. I encourage you to play around with all of the fun and amazing shapes you can make with the stitch-and-flip method. I can't wait to see your finished projects!

Happy sewing!

~ Shelley

The Stitch-and-Flip Lone Star Method

A few years ago, I set out to find a way to make traditional Lone Star quilts without all the diamond pieces and inset seams. I found that many quilters (myself included) just didn't want to mess with all the fuss and frustration that came along with the special techniques needed to make these quilts. With quite a bit of experimentation, I developed a way to make these gorgeous quilts using my favorite stitch-and-flip piecing technique and basic building blocks. This book is filled with fun variations.

SIMPLIFYING THE LONE STAR PATTERN

As a designer, I love developing quilts that appear to be geometrically complex but can easily be assembled with simple shapes and traditional straight-edged piecing. I typically draw my quilt mock-ups first, and then lay the whole thing over graph paper to figure out how to actually put the quilt together. The grid helps me recognize basic geometric shapes that I can then easily replicate with simple quilt blocks.

So, naturally, when I set out to simplify the Lone Star quilt, I started with a basic Lone Star shape against a grid. Sure enough, once I stopped thinking about the quilt in terms of diamonds and started looking for familiar shapes, I began to see a whole lot of half-square-triangle units.

Now, you could absolutely make a Lone Star quilt with nothing but half-square-triangle units, but that requires lots of extra cutting and sewing. When I design quilts, I'm looking for the simplest, most economical way to transform basic shapes into something complex. I prefer to simplify my quilt blocks as much as I can, but at the same time, I like to keep my fabric units as unbroken as possible. Larger pieces not only let me show off my prints, but they also cut down on the number of pieces I have to cut and sew back together again. This, in turn, means I can reduce the number of seam intersections I have to match.

Once I started merging half-square-triangle units, I began to see familiar flying-geese and half-log-cabin units, both of which are super easy to put together using my favorite stitch-and-flip method. Star tips were a little puzzling at first. They could be made by sewing together solid squares and half-square-triangle units, but I still felt like that was using a lot of extra, unnecessarily small pieces. With

a little experimentation, I realized that I could use the same stitch-and-flip corner method to join rectangles set at perpendicular angles. When sewn together and pressed, they mimicked diamonds *without actually using diamonds!*

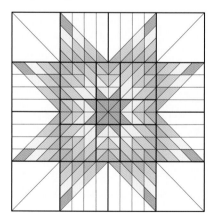

Star Tip block

Half-Log-Cabin block

Flying Geese block

So, there it was—a simple, easy way to make a stunning Lone Star quilt with stitch-and-flip techniques and only three blocks! The more I played around with variations of the Star Tip block, the Half-Log-Cabin block, and the Flying Geese block, the more fun and unique ways I found to use these building blocks to create additional designs.

STITCH-AND-FLIP UNITS

The basic idea behind a stitch-and-flip unit is to sew a smaller square to a larger base square or rectangle at a 45° angle, trim the excess fabric, and then fold over the smaller square to create a corner triangle. You can expand upon this by sewing multiple rectangles to a base piece to create a mock diamond unit. This method eliminates all triangles and bias edges, and in addition to being super speedy to make, it yields accurately sized blocks that are much less likely to become wonky or distorted than with other construction methods.

The following stitch-and-flip units are the pieces needed to make the building blocks, which we'll talk about more on page 13. These essentials will get you on your way to making fabulous quilts that have the complex look of a Lone Star quilt without as much work.

STITCH-AND-FLIP CORNER

The most basic stitch-and-flip unit is the stitch-and-flip corner. It's a very simple and efficient way to add a triangle to a unit.

To make a stitch-and-flip corner, draw a diagonal line from corner to corner on the wrong side of a square. Pin the marked square to its base unit, right sides together, paying careful attention to the placement of the square and the orientation of the stitching line. Stitch on the marked line and then trim the excess fabric ¼" from the stitched line. Press the resulting triangle away from the base unit.

Find Your Own Stitch-and-Flip Rhythm

Some people like to draw diagonal lines on their squares before pinning them to the background pieces, while others prefer to pin and then draw. Still others (who are quite confident with the stitch-and-flip method) skip the lines altogether. Personally, if I draw diagonal lines at all, I prefer to place pieces right sides together first and then mark the diagonal line. That way, I'm less likely to rotate seams incorrectly when I start to sew them.

If you want to skip the pinning part like I do, use a little dab of glue to affix the square to the background piece. Make sure to glue the area that you intend to trim off anyway—and you'll need to plan on tossing or recycling your scraps, because the glued bits won't work for another project.

Before beginning any of the projects in this book, experiment a bit and find the methods that work best for you, your sewing station setup, and your quilting style. There isn't a wrong way! ✹

FLYING-GEESE UNITS

A flying-geese unit can be made using a rectangle and two squares. Stitch, trim, and press a square to the left end of the rectangle and then repeat on the right end, orienting the stitching lines so they point toward the middle of the upper edge.

HOUSE UNITS

Square or rectangular "house" units can be made using the same process that creates a flying-geese unit, only you'll be using two squares for the corners and stitching them to a larger rectangle or square.

Square house unit   Rectangle house unit

HALF-SQUARE-TRIANGLE UNITS

Several of the building blocks use half-square-triangle (HST) units, which are just another version of a stitch-and-flip unit. While these units can easily be made by sewing two triangles together, you can use the following method to completely bypass those bias edges.

Draw a diagonal line from corner to corner on the wrong side of one square. Pin the marked square right sides together on top of another square of the same size. Sew ¼" from both sides of the drawn line, and then cut the squares apart on the drawn line and press in the direction indicated to make two identical HST units.

LEFT- AND RIGHT-LEANING DIAMOND UNITS

Both the Half-Log-Cabin and Star Tip building blocks use left- and right-leaning diamond units. They're constructed by sewing rectangles together at perpendicular angles, trimming off the excess, and then pressing the pieces out before repeating to add additional rectangles. All the various pieces are assigned letters in the cutting instructions for each project to simplify assembly. Once all the rectangles have been joined, stitch-and-flip corners are often added to one or both ends. The trick to assembling these left- and right-leaning units is remembering which direction to sew.

Press Often

You might be tempted to sew together the rectangles in a right- or left-leaning unit all at once, before doing any trimming and pressing. In my experience, however, it's best to stitch, trim, and press each piece before adding the next. This helps you maintain nice, straight edges on your block as you piece and press. Saving the trimming and pressing to do last in one fell swoop typically results in units that wing up or down at either end. It's very challenging to tame them back into straight-edged units! ✳

Left-Leaning Units

Work left-leaning diamond units from *left to right*.

1. Pin (or glue baste) a B rectangle right sides together at a perpendicular angle to the *right end* of an A rectangle as shown on page 12. Make sure that the corners are aligned, and then mark the diagonal sewing line from the top-left corner of the B rectangle to the bottom-right corner of

Stitch-and-Flip Trimmings

Stitch-and-flip sewing techniques are fantastic for quick, precise blocks, but they do result in corner trimmings. With some projects, such as the Wavelength quilt (page 69), the trimmings yield pieces that are the perfect size to be used in other projects. As you're piecing the blocks for that quilt, you can even sew a second seam on each of the corners. That way, when you trim off the corners, you're left with pieces that have already been stitched into a half-square-triangle unit. You can use these leftovers in any project that requires half-square-triangle units of the finished size. Or trim them to a smaller size.

Just in case you need a little inspiration, I've included instructions on page 78 for a quilt using these units. The pattern takes advantage of the trimmings from Wavelength!

Smaller trimmings are useful as bits and bobs for future quilts, as scraps for leader-and-ender projects, or for tiny hexagons or other English-paper-piecing endeavors. You can even hand them off to your guild mates for charity projects! My boys love whisking away my clipped triangle corners and gluing them onto construction paper to make mosaics or paper quilts. Their teachers are happy to incorporate leftovers into classroom art projects, and our local art-recycling studio is always thrilled with donations they can use in their workshops. The possibilities for taking advantage of these triangle trimmings just go on and on.

the A rectangle. Stitch on the drawn line, trim the excess fabric ¼" from the stitching line, and press toward B.

2. Still working from *left to right,* pin the C rectangle at a perpendicular angle to the right edge of the B rectangle. Draw the seamline, stitch, trim, and press toward C.

 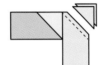

3. Continue to work from *left to right* to add any additional rectangles, and then use the stitch-and-flip corners method (page 9) to add the D and E squares at the ends to finish the unit.

Right-Leaning Units

The right-leaning diamond units are assembled in the exact same way as the left-leaning units, except they're worked from *right to left.* All rectangles are pinned, marked, and sewn together with diagonal seams, and then they're pressed toward the left. Any stitch-and-flip corners are added to the ends once all the rectangles have been sewn together.

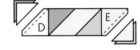 

Alternate Versions

There are multiple variations of left- and right-leaning units, with different numbers of squares and rectangles. Some of your units may have only a stitch-and-flip square on each end, with the seamlines going in the same direction. ✸

MAKING THE BUILDING BLOCKS

Now that you know how to make all the individual stitch-and-flip units, let's look at how the building blocks are assembled. This is the easy part!

FLYING GEESE BUILDING BLOCK

The Flying Geese building block is assembled by sewing several flying-geese units together in a column, with all the triangle tips or "beaks" pointing in the same direction.

Flying Geese building block

Several of the quilts in this book use a combination of flying-geese units and rectangular or square house units joined into a column; once again, all the triangle tips are oriented the same way.

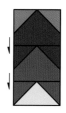 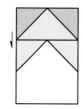

Flying Geese building block variations

While the seam allowances of flying-geese columns typically are pressed away from the points, I've chosen to press the seam allowances of these building blocks toward the points. This permits the seams to nest very nicely with their neighbors.

HALF-LOG-CABIN BUILDING BLOCK

The Half-Log-Cabin building blocks in this book use various combinations of solid squares, half-square-triangle units, solid rectangles with one stitch-and-flip corner, and left- and right-leaning units.

To construct the Half-Log-Cabin building block, start with a solid square and alternate adding units to the right edge and then the bottom edge, pressing after each addition, until the block is complete.

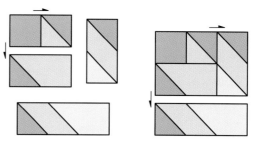

Half-Log-Cabin building block

Several of the quilts in this book use a variation of the building block that is made with a larger starting square, only one unit on the right edge, and only one unit on the bottom edge.

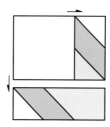

Log Cabin building block variation

STAR TIP BUILDING BLOCK

The Star Tip building blocks are assembled with the same left- and right-leaning units used in our Half-Log-Cabin building block, usually combined with a few solid rectangles that have stitch-and-flip corners. The left- or right-leaning units, along with the rectangles, are simply sewn together into columns, and the seam allowances are pressed open or as directed by the arrows in the assembly diagrams.

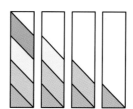 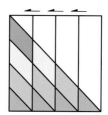

Star Tip blocks are constructed in mirrored pairs, joined either during block construction or during assembly of the quilt top.

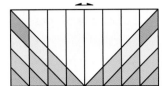

Star Tip building blocks

JOINING PIECES

While the stitch-and-flip method eliminates quite a bit of the fussiness of seam alignment, it's still very important that you take the time to match up your seams before sewing your blocks together. Precision piecing and pinning definitely aren't tricky, but getting things positioned correctly does take a little bit of time. It's time well spent, though, I promise!

To get your stitch-and-flip blocks to line up nicely with their neighbors, you first have to find the "sweet spots" where two seams are supposed to align. If it helps, try marking your ¼" seam allowance along the edge of the wrong side of the block using a fabric pencil or heat-soluble marker. The points where your existing seams intersect this marked line are the exact points where your seams should align—in other words, the sweet spots.

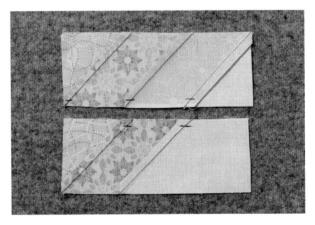

Mark seam intersections on adjoining units.

To assemble, place a pin directly through the sweet spot from wrong side to right side on your first unit. Then, pass the same pin through the sweet spot from right side to wrong side on your second unit. Leave the pin dangling as shown (rather than securing it) for greatest accuracy.

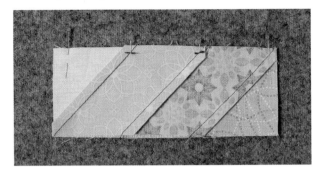

Push a pin through the sweet spots of two units to align the seams.

Carefully sew the seam, making sure that your seam passes through the exact place that you've marked with your pin. Sew right up to the pin, but please don't sew *over* it!

When you open the pieces, you should find perfectly aligned seams.

Occasionally, your points won't line up and you may have to fudge a little. Rather than pinning from one end of the block to the other, start at the center and work your way outward. This often alleviates a lot of problems.

With all the blocks in this book, *be more concerned with lining up your seams perfectly than lining up your edges perfectly.* If your seams are aligned, don't worry if your edges are a tiny bit off. Either gently ease them into place, or just leave them a little uneven, because they'll get buried in the seams anyway.

STITCH-AND-FLIP SUCCESS

I often hear from my students that they're not fans of the stitch-and-flip method . . . until they get the hang of it, and then they're in love and never look back! Getting comfortable with the technique does take a little bit of practice, but here are a few tips to set yourself up for success.

Practice makes perfect. If you're new to the stitch-and-flip method, my advice is to practice, practice, practice! Make a few test blocks before you start with your "real" fabric and your "real" blocks. It might feel a little foreign or strange when you first start, but I promise that if you stick with it, things will click into place.

Mark carefully. Use a fabric-marking pencil or heat-soluble fabric marker to draw your diagonal lines. You don't want any of the markings showing through to the front of your project. Once you're feeling super confident with the stitch-and-flip method, try streamlining your construction process even further by making your units without the extra step of drawing your stitching lines. See "Ditch the Pencil" at right.

Remedy ripples. Does one of your blocks have a bit of a ripple to it once it's pinned in place? Often, this can be remedied by *gently* easing the smaller block into place to match the larger one as you sew. If your sewing machine has a dual-feed feature, this is the time to use it. If it doesn't, sew with the rippled block on the bottom and your feed dogs will help ease the excess in as you sew.

Make tiny adjustments. If you find that you're not happy with the way the units have matched up or you have a bit of a pucker in your seam after sewing, *do not rip out the entire seam!* Instead, pop open five to six stitches on either side of the problem area, and then re-pin, re-sew, and re-press! This will almost always fix the problem.

Ditch the Pencil

When you're ready to use a mark-free method, just extend your sewing line outward from your needle along the machine bed using one of these methods.

Painter's tape. The simplest way to extend a line from your needle to your sewing-machine bed is to place a piece of painter's tape on your machine bed, as shown below, lining up the edge of the tape with the needle. Be sure to use tape that will not leave a sticky residue behind.

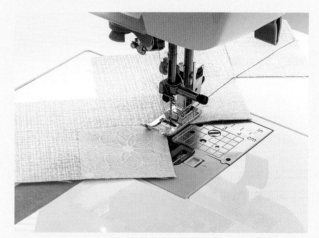

When your sewing line is established, place the unit so that the first corner aligns with the needle and the opposite corner aligns with the guide. Start sewing, and as the fabric moves through the machine, keep that last corner in line with the sewing guide.

Machine aids. Some machines, like my Bernina B770QE, already have a sewing line marked on the machine bed or extension table. Some machines even have fancy laser lights that project the sewing line onto your fabric. I've also seen clever quilters mount simple laser beams onto their machines to mark their sewing lines. Do an online search for "sewing machine laser guide" to learn more.

Plastic guides. If your machine doesn't have a built-in guide and you don't want to mess with lasers or tape, try a product like Quilt in a Day's Sew Straight guide. It's a piece of clear plastic with a marked stitching line, plus some additional diagonal guidelines. It sticks to the bed of your machine or extension table for a temporary guide.

BEFORE YOU BEGIN

Before you start cutting your fabric and piecing your quilts, here are a few more housekeeping items to keep in mind.

FABRIC PREPARATION

Use quilt-shop–quality fabric. The projects in this book weren't written with directional fabric prints in mind. However, directional prints could work well with any of the *rectangular units* in the projects, because they're all cut in the same manner, and you don't have to worry about lining up your print with the print in a neighboring block.

Prewash your fabric or don't; it's your call. Give the fabric a good, solid pressing before doing any cutting to avoid wonky or rippled units.

If you prefer to use a starch-based product on your fabric, use it *before cutting only!* Pressing a starch-dampened unit after cutting can result in distortion.

TOOLS FOR SUCCESS

There are no specialty tools, templates, or rulers required for any of the projects in this book, but you will need some basic supplies. The Shape Cut ruler and wool pressing mat aren't necessary items, but they sure are handy to have around.

For cutting your fabric, make sure to use a clean, dry, flat rotary-cutting mat, along with any of the basic rulers you already have in your sewing arsenal. Make sure your rotary cutter has a nice sharp blade; if you have to force it or make more than one pass to actually cut through your fabric, it's time for a blade change.

Because precision pinning plays a big role in these projects, I recommend investing in some small, super sharp pins to help you accurately assemble your blocks. I really love my Clover Extra Fine Patchwork pins.

Use a good-quality thread in white or another neutral color. I love working with both Wonderfil's DecoBob cottonized-polyester thread and Aurifil's 50-weight cotton Mako thread.

Keep a small pair of thread snippers next to your machine. You might also need a pair of fabric scissors; I prefer to trim my units by hand instead of using my rotary cutter, because it goes much faster.

June Tailor's Shape Cut ruler is a large, slotted ruler that is laid over the top of the fabric, allowing you to quickly and accurately cut multiple strips or units in a fraction of the time it would take to cut with a traditional ruler.

A large 100% wool mat absorbs the heat from your iron. As you press your block from the front, the absorbed heat in the mat also presses the block from the back, giving you superbly flat blocks. My favorite mat is from Wooly Felted Wonders.

BEST SEWING PRACTICES

This book assumes that you have a basic knowledge of standard quilting practices like cutting fabric with a rotary ruler and cutter, sewing with a ¼" seam, pressing, assembling the quilt top and border, and binding. Here's a quick little punch list, though, with a few things every quilter should keep in mind when beginning a new project!

* Start every new quilt with a fresh needle in your machine.

* Join fabric pieces right sides together using a ¼" seam allowance. Take time to check that the ¼" seam setting on your machine is *a true ¼"*. Make any adjustments before you start your project.

* Press your unit or block each time you add a new element. Arrows in the assembly diagrams indicate suggested pressing directions, but they're just that—suggestions. Listen to your block if it's telling you that it wants to go another way.

* Press blocks with a dry iron and try to avoid pushing the fabric around with the iron; this stretches and distorts your blocks!

* The blocks in each pattern are set up so most of the seam allowances will nest together during assembly, but not all will nest, and that's OK!

LET'S GET STARTED!

Are you ready to dive in? The quilts in this book go from easiest to more challenging, so I recommend starting with the first project, Baby Star (page 19). This easy project will walk you through the construction of a basic Lone Star quilt using the building blocks (see page 13).

The remainder of the projects use different combinations and variations of these building blocks to create a variety of Lone Star–inspired runners, pillows, and quilts. Each pattern includes instructions for making an exact replica of the featured quilt, and some projects include alternate layouts showing you even more projects that can be made using the same blocks.

I've classified the projects into three groups based on the following skill levels, which you can easily identify with the star rating:

Confident Beginner

Intermediate

Advanced

Don't let the rating frighten you! As the quilts increase in difficulty, that just means the pieces get smaller and there are more pieces to assemble and more seams to line up. All the quilts, however, are based on the same building blocks, so with careful cutting, precise piecing, and a bit of practice, you'll be ready to make any of the projects in this book in no time.

Baby Star

Need a quick quilt for that upcoming arrival or special event? While Baby Star is the perfect size for a baby or toddler, it's equally appealing to just about every age and gender. Ideal for many occasions, it's also great for your first foray into stitch-and-flip Lone Star quilts.

SKILL LEVEL:

FINISHED QUILT SIZE: 40½" × 40½"

FINISHED BLOCK SIZES:

- Flying Geese block: 4" × 6"
- Half-Log-Cabin block: 6" × 6"
- Star Tip block: 8" × 16"

MATERIALS

Yardage is based on 42"-wide fabric. Fat quarters are 18" × 21".

 1 fat quarter of small-scale white floral for blocks

 1 fat quarter of dark coral large-scale floral for blocks

 1 fat quarter of peach floral for blocks

 ½ yard of medium coral strawberry print for blocks

 1¼ yards of white textural print for background and border

 ¾ yard of medium coral clamshell print for blocks and binding

 1 fat quarter of medium-scale white floral for blocks

2⅝ yards of fabric for backing

47" × 47" square of batting

CUTTING

All measurements include ¼"-wide seam allowances. Label your pieces as you cut. During block assembly, each piece will be referred to by the letter following the dimensions of the piece.

From the small-scale white floral, cut:
1 strip, 4½" × 21"; crosscut into 8 rectangles, 2½" × 4½" (A)
2 strips, 2½" × 21"; crosscut into 12 squares, 2½" × 2½" (D)

From the dark coral large-scale floral, cut:
2 strips, 4½" × 21"; crosscut into:
    1 square, 4½" × 4½" (Q)
    8 rectangles, 2½" × 4½" (O)
1 strip, 2½" × 21"; crosscut into 8 squares, 2½" × 2½" (B)

From the peach floral, cut:
2 strips, 4½" × 21"; crosscut into 16 rectangles, 2½" × 4½" (C)
1 strip, 2⅞" × 21"; crosscut into 2 squares, 2⅞" × 2⅞" (G)
1 strip, 2½" × 21"; crosscut into 8 squares, 2½" × 2½" (F)

Continued on page 20

Continued from page 19

From the medium coral strawberry print, cut:

1 strip, 4½" × 42"; crosscut into:

    4 rectangles, 2½" × 4½" (E)

    2 squares, 2⅞" × 2⅞" (H)

3 strips, 2½" × 42"; crosscut into 48 squares,

    2½" × 2½" (I)

From the white textural print, cut:

4 strips, 4½" × 42"; crosscut into:

    2 strips, 4½" × 32½"

    2 strips, 4½" × 40½"

1 strip, 8½" × 42"; crosscut into 4 squares,

    8½" × 8½" (R)

5 strips, 2½" × 42"; crosscut into:

    8 rectangles, 2½" × 8½" (J)

    8 rectangles, 2½" × 6½" (K)

    8 rectangles, 2½" × 4½" (M)

    8 squares, 2½" × 2½" (P)

From the medium coral clamshell print, cut:

2 strips, 4½" × 42"; crosscut into 24 rectangles,

    2½" × 4½" (L)

5 strips, 2½" × 42"

From the medium-scale white floral, cut:

2 strips, 4½" × 21"; crosscut into 16 rectangles,

    2½" × 4½" (N)

MAKING THE
FLYING GEESE BLOCKS

Use a ¼" seam allowance. Press the seam allowances as indicated by the arrows in the illustrations. Measurements given for assembled pieces include seam allowances.

1. Use the A, C, and E rectangles and the B, D, and F squares to make four sets of three flying-geese units (see page 10). Press. Each unit should measure 2½" × 4½".

Make 4 of each unit,
2½" × 4½".

2. Join one of each step 1 unit to make a Flying Geese block. Press. Repeat to make a total of four blocks measuring 4½" × 6½".

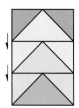

Make 4 Flying Geese blocks,
4½" × 6½".

MAKING THE
HALF-LOG-CABIN BLOCKS

1. Use G and H squares to make four half-square-triangle units (see page 10). Press. Each unit should measure 2½" square.

Make 4 units,
2½" × 2½".

2. Sew D and I squares to the left and right ends of a C rectangle as shown to make a right-leaning unit (see page 12). Press and repeat to make a total of four units measuring 2½" × 4½".

Make 4 units,
2½" × 4½".

3. Sew an I square to the left end of a C rectangle to make a stitch-and-flip corner (see page 9). Press. Repeat to make a total of four units measuring 2½" × 4½".

Make 4 units,
2½" × 4½".

By Shelley Cavanna; quilted by Darby Myers

4. Use A and C rectangles and an I square to make a left-leaning unit (see page 10). Press and repeat to make a total of four units measuring 2½" × 6½".

Make 4 units,
2½" × 6½".

5. Join one unit each from steps 1–4 with an I square to make a Half-Log-Cabin block (see page 13). Press and repeat to make a total of four blocks measuring 6½" square.

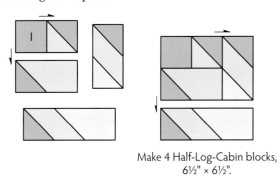

Make 4 Half-Log-Cabin blocks,
6½" × 6½".

MAKING THE STAR TIP BLOCKS

1. Use I–P pieces to make four sets of four right-leaning units and four left-leaning units. Press. Each unit should measure 2½" × 8½".

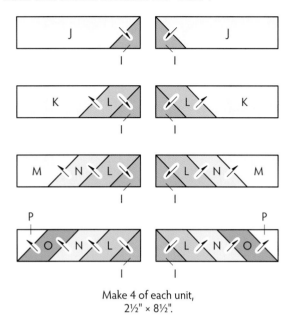

Make 4 of each unit,
2½" × 8½".

2. Join one of each unit from step 1 to make a Star Tip block (see page 13). Press. Repeat to make a total of four blocks measuring 8½" × 16½".

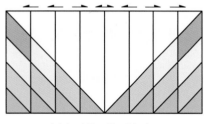

Make 4 Star Tip blocks,
8½" × 16½".

Precision Pinning

For any block with multiple seam intersections, start pinning from the middle of the units outward to ease out any ripples or misaligned sections as you go along. ✳

ASSEMBLING THE QUILT TOP

1. Lay out the Flying Geese blocks, the Half-Log-Cabin blocks, and the Q square in three horizontal rows as shown. Join the pieces in each row. Press. Join the rows to make the star center. Press. The star center should measure 16½" square.

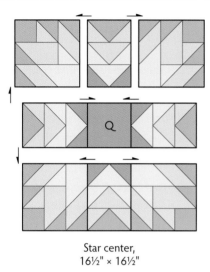

Star center,
16½" × 16½"

2. Arrange the star center, the Star Tip blocks, and the white textural print 8½" squares in three horizontal rows as shown. Join the pieces in each row. Press. Join the rows to complete the quilt center. The quilt center should measure 32½" square.

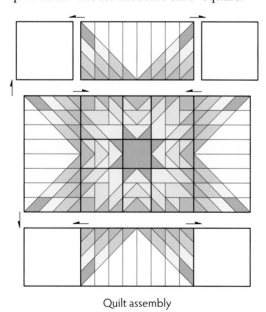

Quilt assembly

3. Join the white textural print 4½" × 32½" strips to the sides of the quilt center. Press the seam allowances toward the strips. Add the white textural print 4½" × 40½" strips to the top and bottom of the quilt center. Press the seam allowances toward the strips. The quilt top should measure 40½" square.

FINISHING

1. Layer the quilt top, batting, and backing. Baste the layers together.

2. Hand or machine quilt as desired. The quilt shown is machine quilted with an allover floral design.

3. Use the medium-light coral 2½"-wide strips to make the binding; attach the binding to the quilt.

Alternate Size

For a larger quilt that finishes at 70½" × 70½", make four baby stars and join them in a two by two arrangement with 2" (finished) sashing and cornerstones. ✻

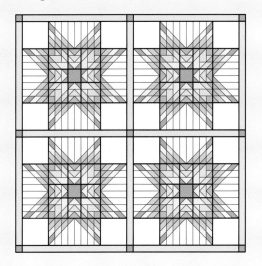

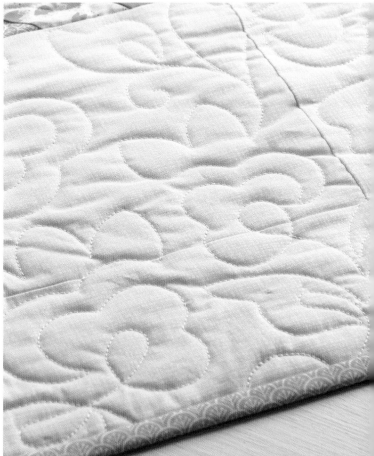

Dandelions

Create curves without curved piecing! The Dandelion blocks are actually mini Lone Star blocks. Pieced using Flying Geese and Half-Log-Cabin building blocks, the blocks create the illusion of rounded edges. The modern setting features four blocks in a graphic, stair-stepped layout, just like dandelions growing in the wild.

SKILL LEVEL:

FINISHED QUILT SIZE: 60½" × 66½"
FINISHED BLOCK SIZE: 15" × 15"

MATERIALS

Yardage is based on 42"-wide fabric. Fat eighths are 9" × 21".

 12 fat eighths of assorted coordinating prints for blocks*

 3 yards of cream textural print for background

 ⅝ yard of coordinating dark print for binding*

4 yards of fabric for backing

67" × 73" rectangle of batting

*To add cohesion, I used a fat eighth of the same dark print used for the binding for either the inner star or middle star in every block. It's a great way to show off your favorite print or color! To follow my lead, 4 of the 12 fat eighths should be from the same fabric used for the binding. Or you can purchase 8 fat eighths and 1 yard total of the binding fabric.

CUTTING

All measurements include ¼"-wide seam allowances. Separate your fat eighths into four sets of three prints: one print for the inner star and the single points of the outer star, one print for the middle star, and one print for the double points of the outer star. (If you didn't purchase separate fat eighths of the binding fabric, cut the binding strips first and then use the remaining fabric to cut the necessary pieces from the leftover binding yardage.) You'll use one set of prints to make each block. Label your pieces as you cut and keep the pieces for each block together. During block assembly, each piece will be referred to by the letter following the dimensions of the piece.

FOR 1 BLOCK

(Cut 4 total.)

From the inner-star print, cut:
1 strip, 4¼" × 21"; crosscut into:
    8 rectangles, 2" × 4¼" (H)
    1 square, 3½" × 3½" (L)
1 strip, 2" × 21"; crosscut into 8 squares, 2" × 2" (B)

From the middle-star print, cut:
1 strip, 3½" × 21"; crosscut into:
    4 rectangles, 2¾" × 3½" (A)
    4 rectangles, 2" × 3½" (J)
2 strips, 2" × 21"; crosscut into 12 squares, 2" × 2" (D)

Continued on page 26

MAKING THE BLOCKS

Use a ¼" seam allowance. Press the seam allowances as indicated by the arrows in the illustrations. Measurements given for assembled pieces include seam allowances.

1. Select the pieces cut for one block.

2. Use the A and C rectangles and the B and D squares to make four of each house unit (see page 10) as shown. Press. Each unit should measure 2¾" × 3½".

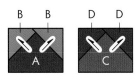

Make 4 of each unit,
2¾" × 3½".

Continued from page 25

From the outer-star print, cut:

1 strip, 3½" × 21"; crosscut into:
  4 rectangles, 2¾" × 3½" (C)
  4 rectangles, 2" × 3½" (I)
2 strips, 2" × 21"; crosscut into 12 squares, 2" × 2" (F)

FOR THE REMAINING PIECES

From the cream textural print, cut:

5 strips, 15½" × 42"; crosscut into:
  1 strip, 15½" × 41"
  2 strips, 15½" × 35"
  1 strip, 15½" × 29"
  1 strip, 15½" × 23"
  2 rectangles, 15½" × 17"
  1 rectangle, 11" × 15½"
4 strips, 3½" × 42"; crosscut into:
  16 squares, 3½" × 3½" (K)
  48 rectangles, 2" × 3½" (E)
2 strips, 2¾" × 42"; crosscut into 32 rectangles,
  2" × 2¾" (G)

From the binding print, cut:

7 strips, 2½" × 42"

3. Use the E rectangles and the F squares to make four flying-geese units (see page 10). Press. Each unit should measure 2" × 3½".

Make 4 units,
2" × 3½".

4. Join one of each unit from steps 2 and 3 to make a Flying Geese variation block. Press. Repeat to make a total of four blocks measuring 3½" × 6½".

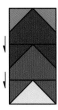

Make 4 Flying Geese variation blocks,
3½" × 6½".

By Shelley Cavanna; quilted by Darby Myers

---

5. Sew an F square to the left end of an E rectangle to make a stitch-and-flip corner (see page 9). Press. Repeat to make a total of four units measuring 2" × 3½".

Make 4 units,
2" × 3½".

6. Make four right-leaning units (see page 12) using G and H rectangles and D squares. Press. Each unit should measure 2" × 5".

Make 4 units,
2" × 5".

7. Use the E and I rectangles to make four left-leaning units that measure 2" × 5" (see page 10). Press.

Make 4 units,
2" × 5".

8. Use G, H, and J rectangles to make four left-leaning units. Press. Each unit should measure 2" × 6½".

Make 4 units,
2" × 6½".

9. Join one unit each from steps 5–8 with a K square to make a Half-Log-Cabin block. Press and repeat to make a total of four blocks measuring 6½" square.

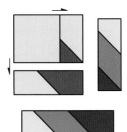 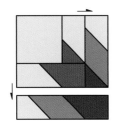

Make 4 Half-Log-Cabin blocks,
6½" × 6½".

10. Lay out the Flying Geese blocks, the Half-Log-Cabin blocks, and the L square in three horizontal rows as shown. Join the pieces in each row. Press. Join the rows. Press. The Dandelion block should measure 15½" square.

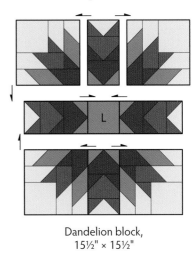

Dandelion block,
15½" × 15½"

11. Repeat steps 2–10 with the remaining sets of prints to make a total of four blocks.

ASSEMBLING THE QUILT TOP

Refer to the quilt assembly diagram to arrange the blocks and cream background pieces in four columns, placing one block in each row as desired. Join the pieces in each row. Press. Join the rows. Press. The quilt top should measure 60½" × 66½".

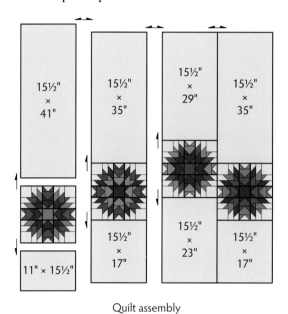

Quilt assembly

FINISHING

1. Layer the quilt top, batting, and backing. Baste the layers together.

2. Hand or machine quilt as desired. The quilt shown is machine quilted with an allover swirl design.

3. Use the dark plum 2½"-wide strips to make the binding; attach the binding to the quilt.

Alternate Layout

For a 60½" square quilt with a more traditional feel, make 16 Dandelion blocks using assorted prints, and join them in a four by four layout. The blocks can be sewn together quickly because there are very few seams to match up, and as a bonus, the background fabric comes together to make an interesting pineapple-like secondary pattern! ✹

Pinwheels

Grab a bundle of precut 10" squares or 2½" strips and minimize the cutting for Pinwheels. You'll have enough fabric left over to make one additional block, which is the perfect size for a matching throw pillow! To add visual interest, try using a textile with texture such as a linen or yarn-dyed cotton, like the tan linen I used for the sashing.

SKILL LEVEL:

FINISHED QUILT SIZE: 64½" × 64½"
FINISHED BLOCK SIZE: 16" × 16"

MATERIALS

Yardage is based on 42"-wide fabric.

 40 precut squares, 10" × 10", OR 40 precut strips, 2½" × 42", of assorted prints for blocks and sashing cornerstones

 1⅔ yards of white textural print for block backgrounds

 1 yard of tan textural print for sashing

 1 yard of yellow floral for border

 ⅝ yard of coral floral for binding

4 yards of fabric for backing

71" × 71" square of batting

CUTTING

All measurements include ¼"-wide seam allowances. Separate your 10" squares or 2½"-wide strips into nine sets of four prints: one dark print, two medium prints, and one light print. You'll use one set to make each block. Label your pieces as you cut and keep the pieces for each block together. During block assembly, each piece will be referred to by the letter following the dimensions of the piece.

FOR 1 BLOCK

(Cut 9 total.)

From 1 medium print, cut:
4 rectangles, 2½" × 4½" (A)
8 squares, 2½" × 2½" (D)

From the dark print, cut:
1 square, 4½" × 4½", OR 2 rectangles, 2½" × 4½", sewn together to make a 4½" square
8 squares, 2½" × 2½" (B)

From the remaining medium print, cut:
8 rectangles, 2½" × 4½" (E)

From the light print, cut:
4 rectangles, 2½" × 4½" (H)
4 squares, 2½" × 2½" (F)

Continued on page 32

Pieced by Shelley Cavanna and Rene´ Stout; quilted by Darby Myers

Continued from page 31

FOR THE REMAINING PIECES

From the white textural print, cut:
9 strips, 4½" × 42"; crosscut into 72 squares,
    4½" × 4½" (C)
5 strips, 2½" × 42"; crosscut into 72 squares,
    2½" × 2½" (G)

From the tan textural print, cut:
12 strips, 2½" × 42"; crosscut into 24 rectangles,
    2½" × 16½"

From the prints used for the blocks, cut a *total* of:
16 squares, 2½" × 2½"

From the yellow floral, cut:
7 strips, 4½" × 42"

From the coral floral, cut:
7 strips, 2½" × 42"

MAKING THE BLOCKS

Use a ¼" seam allowance. Press the seam allowances as indicated by the arrows in the illustrations. Measurements given for assembled pieces include seam allowances.

1. Select the pieces cut for one block.

2. Make four flying-geese units (see page 10) using A rectangles and B squares. Press. Each unit should measure 2½" × 4½".

Make 4 units,
2½" × 4½".

3. Make four house units (see page 10) using C and D squares. Press. Each unit should measure 4½" square.

Make 4 units,
2½" × 4½".

4. Join one unit each from steps 2 and 3 to make a Flying Geese variation block. Press and repeat to make a total of four blocks measuring 4½" × 6½".

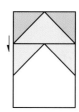

Make 4 Flying Geese variation blocks,
4½" × 6½".

5. Make four right-leaning units (see page 12) using E rectangles and F and G squares. Press. Each unit should measure 2½" × 4½".

Make 4 units,
2½" × 4½".

6. Make four left-leaning units (see page 10) using E and H rectangles and G squares. Press. Each unit should measure 2½" × 6½".

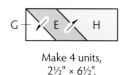

Make 4 units,
2½" × 6½".

7. Join one unit each from steps 5 and 6 with a C square to make a Half-Log-Cabin block. Press. Repeat to make a total of four blocks measuring 6½" square.

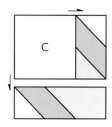

Make 4 Half-Log-Cabin blocks,
6½" × 6½".

8. Lay out the Flying Geese blocks, the Half-Log-Cabin blocks, and the dark 4½" square in three horizontal rows. Join the pieces in each row. Press. Join the rows. Press. The Pinwheel block should measure 16½" square.

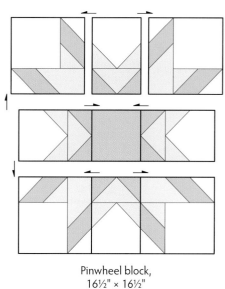

Pinwheel block,
16½" × 16½"

9. Repeat steps 1–8 to make a total of nine blocks.

ASSEMBLING THE QUILT TOP

1. Refer to the quilt assembly diagram below to lay out the blocks, the tan 2½" × 16½" sashing rectangles, and the assorted print 2½" square sashing cornerstones in three block rows and four sashing rows as shown. When you're satisfied with the color placement, sew the pieces in each row together. Press. Join the rows. Press. The quilt center should measure 56½" square.

2. Join three yellow floral 4½" × 42" strips end to end to make one long strip. Press the seam allowances open. From the pieced strip, cut two 4½" × 56½" strips and sew them to the sides of the quilt center. Press the seam allowances toward the strips. Join the four remaining yellow floral 4½" × 42" strips end to end and press as before. From the pieced strip, cut two 4½" × 64½" strips and sew them to the top and bottom edges of the quilt center. Press the seam allowances toward the strips. The quilt top should measure 64½" square.

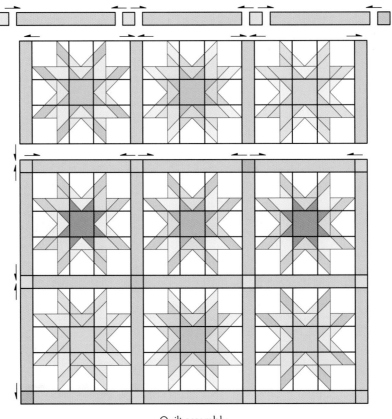

Quilt assembly

FINISHING

1. Layer the quilt top, batting, and backing. Baste the layers together.

2. Hand or machine quilt as desired. The quilt shown is machine quilted with an allover design of four interconnecting leaves that form a grid across the quilt top.

3. Use the coral floral 2½"-wide strips to make the binding; attach the binding to the quilt.

Alternate Project

Most sets of precut 10" squares or 2½" strips include at least 40 pieces of fabric, which is enough to make 10 Pinwheel blocks. Because only nine blocks are needed for the quilt top, you can use the remaining four pieces of fabric from your bundle to make a tenth block to turn into a matching pillow. Add sashing and cornerstone squares to the perimeter of the block and you'll have a 20" pillow that complements your quilt perfectly! ✳

Fletching Table Runner

Mastering the chevron, which is a not-so-distant cousin to the Lone Star, has never been easier when you use left- and right-leaning units to do the work. Set your sights on your favorite color scheme, and hitting your target for making the zigzags will be effortless with stitch-and-flip techniques!

SKILL LEVEL:

FINISHED RUNNER SIZE: 16½" × 64½"

FINISHED BLOCK SIZE: 16" × 16"

MATERIALS

Yardage is based on 42"-wide fabric. Fat quarters are 18" × 21".

 ⅝ yard of medium blue floral for blocks and binding

 1 fat quarter of light blue leaf-and-vine print for blocks

 1 fat quarter of red-on-white floral for blocks

 1 fat quarter of dark blue floral for blocks

 1 fat quarter of red-on-white vine print for blocks

 1 fat quarter of red floral for blocks

 1 fat quarter of dark blue vine print for blocks

 1 fat quarter of red textural print for blocks

 ¾ yard of cream print for background

1⅓ yards of fabric for backing

23" × 71" rectangle of batting

CUTTING

All measurements include ¼"-wide seam allowances. Label your pieces as you cut. During block assembly, each piece will be referred to by the letter following the dimensions of the piece. For a scrappier-looking runner, mix in as many various prints for pieces A–H as you'd like!

From the medium blue floral, cut:
1 strip, 4½" × 42"; crosscut into 16 rectangles,
    2½" × 4½" (A)
5 strips, 2½" × 42"

From the light blue leaf-and-vine print, cut:
2 strips, 4½" × 21"; crosscut into 16 rectangles,
    2½" × 4½" (B)

From the red-on-white floral, cut:
2 strips, 4½" × 21"; crosscut into 16 rectangles,
    2½" × 4½" (C)

From the dark blue floral, cut:
2 strips, 4½" × 21"; crosscut into 16 rectangles,
    2½" × 4½" (D)

From the red-on-white vine print, cut:
2 strips, 4½" × 21"; crosscut into 16 rectangles,
    2½" × 4½" (E)

From the red floral, cut:
2 strips, 4½" × 21"; crosscut into 16 rectangles,
    2½" × 4½" (F)

From the dark blue vine print, cut:
2 strips, 4½" × 21"; crosscut into 16 rectangles,
    2½" × 4½" (G)

From the red textural print, cut:
2 strips, 4½" × 21"; crosscut into 16 rectangles,
    2½" × 4½" (H)

From the cream print, cut:
9 strips, 2½" × 42"; crosscut into:
    16 rectangles, 2½" × 8½" (I)
    16 rectangles, 2½" × 6½" (J)
    16 rectangles, 2½" × 4½" (K)
    16 squares, 2½" × 2½" (L)

MAKING THE BLOCKS

Use a ¼" seam allowance. Press the seam allowances as indicated by the arrows in the illustrations. Measurements given for assembled pieces include seam allowances.

1. Using A–K rectangles and L squares, make four of each right-leaning unit (see page 12). Press. Each unit should measure 2½" × 16½".

Make 4 of each unit,
2½" × 16½".

2. Join one of each step 1 unit. Press. Repeat to make a total of four units measuring 8½" × 16½".

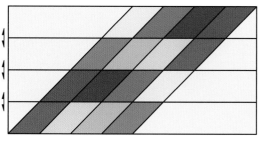

Make 4 units,
8½" × 16½".

By Shelley Cavanna

3. Using A–K rectangles and L squares, make four of each left-leaning unit (see page 10). Each unit should measure 2½" × 16½".

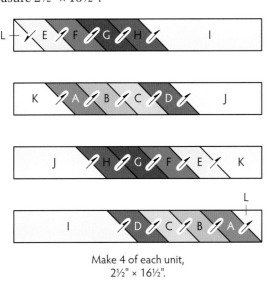

Make 4 of each unit,
2½" × 16½".

4. Join one of each step 3 unit. Press. Repeat to make a total of four units measuring 8½" × 16½".

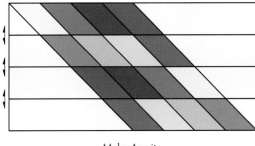

Make 4 units,
8½" × 16½".

5. Join one unit each from steps 2 and 4 as shown. Press. Repeat to make a total of four Fletching blocks measuring 16½" square.

Make 4 blocks,
16½" × 16½".

ASSEMBLING THE TABLE RUNNER

Join the blocks in one horizontal row. Press. The runner top should measure 16½" × 64½".

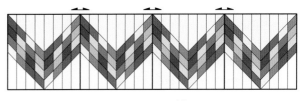

Runner assembly

FINISHING

1. Layer the runner top, batting, and backing. Baste the layers together.

2. Hand or machine quilt as desired. The runner shown is machine quilted ¼" from each side of the seamlines.

3. Use the medium blue floral 2½"-wide strips to make the binding; attach the binding to the runner.

Alternate Layout

For a quick and easy 64½" square quilt, make a total of 16 Fletching blocks and sew them into four rows of four blocks each. For a scrappier quilt, cut the A–H rectangles from as many different prints as you'd like!

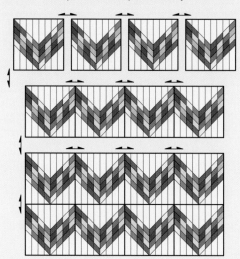

Dream Catcher

Are you dreaming, or are the blocks layered on top of each other? Neither! I love Dream Catcher because geometric shapes create the illusion of depth, so it only appears that the blocks are layered. While the design looks complex, it's actually easy to achieve this layered look using what I like to call Double Stitch-and-Flip blocks. These double blocks are just as easy to piece as half-square-triangle units; you just stitch-and-flip them twice!

SKILL LEVEL: ✳ ✳

FINISHED QUILT SIZE: 90½" × 90½"

FINISHED BLOCK SIZE: 10" × 10"

MATERIALS

Yardage is based on 42"-wide fabric.

 1 yard of light mulberry print for blocks

 1⅝ yards of dark mulberry print for blocks

 ⅝ yard of dark aqua floral for blocks

 1⅓ yards of light aqua floral for blocks

 1⅝ yards of small-scale navy print for blocks

 1⅔ yards of navy textural print for blocks and binding

 ⅞ yard of medium aqua wavy lines print for blocks

 1⅜ yards of medium gray wavy lines print for blocks

 4⅝ yards of light gray textural print for block backgrounds and border

8¼ yards of fabric for backing

99" × 99" square of batting

CUTTING

All measurements include ¼"-wide seam allowances. Label your pieces as you cut. During block assembly, each piece will be referred to by the letter following the dimensions of the piece.

From the light mulberry print, cut:
3 strips, 3⅜" × 42"; crosscut into 24 squares,
    3⅜" × 3⅜" (A)
7 strips, 3" × 42"; crosscut into 80 squares, 3" × 3" (D)

From the dark mulberry print, cut:
6 strips, 5½" × 42"; crosscut into 72 rectangles,
    3" × 5½" (F)
3 strips, 3⅜" × 42"; crosscut into 26 squares,
    3⅜" × 3⅜" (B)
3 strips, 3" × 42"; crosscut into 28 squares, 3" × 3" (L)

From the dark aqua floral, cut:
6 strips, 3" × 42"; crosscut into 40 rectangles,
    3" × 5½" (C)

From the light aqua floral, cut:
6 strips, 5½" × 42"; crosscut into 76 rectangles,
    3" × 5½" (G)
1 strip, 3⅜" × 42"; crosscut into 4 squares,
    3⅜" × 3⅜" (P)
2 strips, 3" × 42"; crosscut into 20 squares, 3" × 3" (E)

From the small-scale navy print, cut:
3 strips, 5½" × 42"; crosscut into 32 rectangles,
    3" × 5½" (T)
12 strips, 3" × 42"; crosscut into 144 squares,
    3" × 3" (H)

From the navy textural print, cut:
4 strips, 5½" × 42"; crosscut into 48 rectangles,
    3" × 5½" (J)
2 strips, 3" × 42"; crosscut into 16 squares, 3" × 3" (I)
10 strips, 2½" × 42"

From the medium aqua wavy lines print, cut:
3 strips, 5½" × 42"; crosscut into 36 rectangles,
    3" × 5½" (M)
3 strips, 3⅜" × 42"; crosscut into 26 squares,
    3⅜" × 3⅜" (K)

From the medium gray wavy lines print, cut:
5 strips, 5½" × 42"; crosscut into 64 rectangles,
    3" × 5½" (Q)
2 strips, 3¾" × 42"; crosscut into 16 squares,
    3¾" × 3¾" (N)
3 strips, 3" × 42"; crosscut into 32 squares, 3" × 3" (U)

From the light gray textural print, cut:
6 strips, 10½" × 42"; crosscut into:
    4 rectangles, 10½" × 20½"
    8 squares, 10½" × 10½"
12 strips, 5½" × 42"; crosscut *3 of the strips* into
    32 rectangles, 3" × 5½" (S)
2 strips, 3¾" × 42"; crosscut into 16 squares,
    3¾" × 3¾" (O)
5 strips, 3" × 42"; crosscut into 64 squares, 3" × 3" (R)

About the Blocks

Blocks 1 and 2 follow the construction for Half-Log-Cabin building blocks (see page 13). Because this quilt creates the illusion of stars floating behind stars, the piecing for the remainder of the blocks in the quilt will use a hybrid Half-Log-Cabin/Star Tip block. It's constructed with small, stair-stepped log-cabin units and left- and right-leaning units from the Star Tip building blocks (see page 13). Take the time to align and pin your seam intersections, and press all the seam allowances either open or as directed by the arrows in the assembly diagrams. ✳

MAKING BLOCK 1

Use a ¼" seam allowance. Press the seam allowances as indicated by the arrows in the illustrations. Measurements given for assembled pieces include seam allowances.

1. Using A and B squares, make 20 half-square-triangle units (see page 10). Press. Each unit should measure 3" square. You'll use 12 units for block 1 and four each for blocks 5 and 6.

Make 20 units,
3" × 3".

2. Using C rectangles and D and E squares, make 12 sets of right-leaning units (see page 12). Press. Each unit should measure 3" × 5½".

Make 12 units,
3" × 5½".

3. Using F and G rectangles and H and I squares, make 12 right-leaning units. Press. Each unit should measure 3" × 8".

Make 12 units,
3" × 8".

4. Sew a D square to the left end of an F rectangle to make a stitch-and-flip corner (see page 9). Press. Repeat to make a total of 12 units measuring 3" × 5½".

Make 12 units,
3" × 5½".

5. Using C and G rectangles and D squares, make 12 left-leaning units (see page 10). Press. Each unit should measure 3" × 8".

Make 12 units,
3" × 8".

6. Using F, G, and J rectangles and H squares, make 12 left-leaning units. Press. Each unit should measure 3" × 10½".

Make 12 units,
3" × 10½".

7. Join one unit each from steps 1–6 with an H square to make block 1. Press and repeat to make a total of 12 blocks measuring 10½" square. Set aside the remaining eight A/B half-square-triangle units.

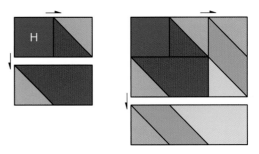

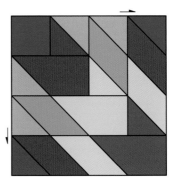

Block 1.
Make 12 blocks,
10½" × 10½".

MAKING BLOCK 2

1. Using A and K squares, make 28 half-square-triangle units. Press. Each unit should measure 3" square. You'll use four units for block 2 and 12 units each for blocks 3 and 4.

Make 28 units,
3" × 3".

2. Using G rectangles and D and L squares, make four right-leaning units. Press. Each unit should measure 3" × 5½".

Make 4 units,
3" × 5½".

3. Using C and M rectangles and H and I squares, make four right-leaning units. Press. Each unit should measure 3" × 8".

Make 4 units,
3" × 8".

4. Sew a D square to the left end of an M rectangle to make a stitch-and-flip corner. Press. Repeat to make a total of four units measuring 3" × 5½".

Make 4 units,
3" × 5½".

5. Using G and F rectangles and D squares, make four left-leaning units. Press. Each unit should measure 3" × 8".

Make 4 units,
3" × 8".

6. Using C, M, and J rectangles and H squares, make four left-leaning units. Press. Each unit should measure 3" × 10½".

Make 4 units,
3" × 10½".

7. Referring to "Half-Log-Cabin Building Block" on page 13, join one unit each from steps 1–6 with an H square to make block 2. Press. Repeat to make a total of four blocks measuring 10½" square. Set aside the remaining 24 A/K half-square-triangle units.

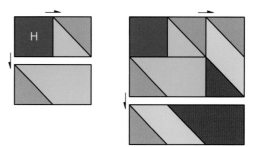

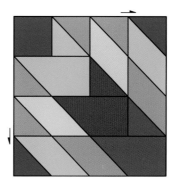

Block 2.
Make 4 blocks,
10½" × 10½".

By Shelley Cavanna; quilted by Cara Cansler

MAKING UNITS
FOR BLOCKS 3–6

The four remaining blocks in this quilt have almost identical coloring. Because they use so many of the same elements, the construction process has been simplified by first assembling some units that will be used in more than one block.

1. Using N and O squares, make 32 half-square-triangle units. Press. Each unit should measure 3⅜" square.

Make 32 units,
3⅜" × 3⅜".

2. Draw a diagonal line from corner to corner on the wrong side of 16 B squares, 12 K squares, and four P squares.

3. Layer a marked B square on top of a half-square-triangle unit from step 1, right sides together. The marked line should run in the opposite direction as the seam of the half-square-triangle unit. Sew ¼" from each side of the drawn line. Cut the squares apart on the marked line to make units 1 and 2. Press. Repeat with the remaining marked B squares to make 16 each of units 1 and 2 measuring 3" square.

Unit 1.
Make 16 units,
3" × 3".

Unit 2.
Make 16 units,
3" × 3".

4. Repeat step 3 with the marked K and P squares and the remaining half-square-triangle units to make 12 each of units 3 and 4 and four each of units 5 and 6.

Unit 3.
Make 12 units,
3" × 3".

Unit 4.
Make 12 units,
3" × 3".

Unit 5.
Make 4 units,
3" × 3".

Unit 6.
Make 4 units,
3" × 3".

5. Using Q rectangles and H and R squares, make 16 sets of right- and left-leaning units for units 7 and 8. Press. Each unit should measure 3" × 5½".

Unit 7.
Make 16 units,
3" × 5½".

Unit 8.
Make 16 units,
3" × 5½".

6. To make unit 9, use Q, S, and T rectangles to make 16 right-leaning units. Press. Sew an H square to the left end of each unit to make a stitch-and-flip corner. Each unit should measure 3" × 10½".

Unit 9.
Make 16 units,
3" × 10½".

7. To make unit 10, use Q, S, and T rectangles to make 16 left-leaning units. Press. Sew an H square to the right end of each unit to make a stitch-and-flip corner. Each unit should measure 3" × 10½".

Unit 10.
Make 16 units,
3" × 10½".

MAKING BLOCK 3

1. Using G rectangles and D and L squares, make 12 right-leaning units. Press. Each unit should measure 3" × 5½".

Make 12 units,
3" × 5½".

2. Using F, J, and M rectangles and H and R squares, make 12 right-leaning units. Press. Each unit should measure 3" × 10½".

Make 12 units,
3" × 10½".

3. Sew a U square to the right end of a unit 1. Press. Join a unit 7 to the top of this unit. Press. Repeat to make a total of 12 units measuring 5½" square.

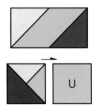

Make 12 units,
5½" × 5½".

4. Sew a unit 4 to the top of one of the A/K half-square-triangle units you set aside from block 2. Press. Join a right-leaning unit from step 1 to the left edge of this unit. Press. Repeat to make a total of 12 units measuring 5½" square.

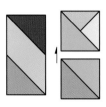

Make 12 units,
5½" × 5½".

5. Sew a unit from step 3 to the top of a unit from step 4. Press. Repeat to make a total of 12 units measuring 5½" × 10½".

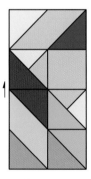

Make 12 units,
5½" × 10½".

6. Sew a unit 10 to the right edge of a unit from step 5. Press. Join a right-leaning unit from step 2 to the left edge of this unit to complete block 3. Press. Make a total of 12 blocks measuring 10½" square. Set aside the remaining 12 A/K half-square-triangle units.

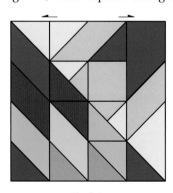

Block 3.
Make 12 blocks,
10½" × 10½".

MAKING BLOCK 4

1. Using G rectangles and D and L squares, make 12 left-leaning units. Press. Each unit should measure 3" × 5½".

Make 12 units,
3" × 5½".

2. Using F, J, and M rectangles and H and R squares, make 12 left-leaning units. Press. Each unit should measure 3" × 10½".

Make 12 units,
3" × 10½".

3. Sew a U square to the left edge of a unit 2. Press. Attach a unit 8 to the top of this unit. Press. Repeat to make a total of 12 units measuring 5½" square.

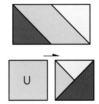 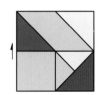

Make 12 units,
5½" × 5½".

4. Attach a unit 3 to the top of an A/K half-square-triangle unit you set aside from block 3. Press. Attach a unit from step 1 to the right edge. Press. Repeat to make a total of 12 units measuring 5½" square.

  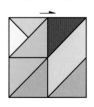

Make 12 units,
5½" × 5½".

5. Join a unit from step 3 to the top of a unit from step 4. Press. Add a unit 9 to the left edge of this unit and a unit from step 2 to the right edge. Press. Repeat to make a total of 12 units measuring 10½" square.

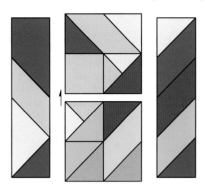

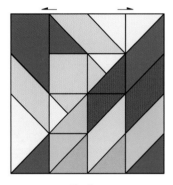

Block 4.
Make 12 blocks,
10½" × 10½".

MAKING BLOCK 5

1. Using C rectangles and D and E squares, make four left-leaning units. Press. Each unit should measure 3" × 5½".

Make 4 units,
3" × 5½".

2. Using F, G, and J rectangles and H and R squares, make four left-leaning units. Press. Each unit should measure 3" × 10½".

Make 4 units,
3" × 10½".

3. Sew a U square to the left edge of a unit 6. Press. Join a unit 8 to the top of this unit. Press. Repeat to make a total of four units measuring 5½" square.

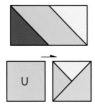

Make 4 units,
5½" × 5½".

4. Sew a unit 1 to the top of an A/B half-square-triangle left over from block 1. Press. Join a unit from step 1 to the right edge of this unit. Press. Repeat to make a total of four units measuring 5½" square.

Make 4 units,
5½" × 5½".

5. Join a step 3 unit to the top of a step 4 unit. Press. Add a unit 9 to the left edge of this unit and a unit from step 2 to the right edge to complete block 5. Press. Repeat to make a total of four blocks measuring 10½" square. Set aside the remaining four A/B half-square-triangle units.

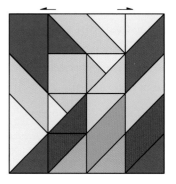

Block 5.
Make 4 blocks,
10½" × 10½".

MAKING BLOCK 6

1. Using C rectangles and D and E squares, make four right-leaning units. Press. Each unit should measure 3" × 5½".

Make 4 units,
3" × 5½".

2. Using F, G, and J rectangles and H and R squares, make four right-leaning units. Press. Each unit should measure 3" × 10½".

Make 4 units,
3" × 10½".

3. Sew a U square to the right edge of a unit 5. Press. Join a unit 7 to the top of this unit. Press. Repeat to make a total of four units measuring 5½" square.

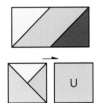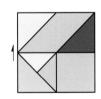

Make 4 units,
5½" × 5½".

4. Sew a unit 2 to the top of an A/B half-square-triangle unit you set aside from block 5. Press. Join a unit from step 1 to the left edge of this unit. Repeat to make a total of four units measuring 5½" square.

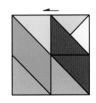

Make 4 units,
5½" × 5½".

5. Join a unit from step 3 to the top of a unit from step 4. Press. Add a unit from step 2 to the left edge of this unit and a unit 10 to the right edge to complete block 6. Press. Repeat to make a total of four blocks measuring 10½" square.

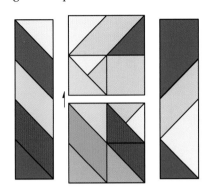

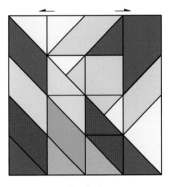

Block 6.
Make 4 blocks,
10½" × 10½".

Speed Up Assembly with Chain Piecing!

Sew together your first pair of units but don't stop when you come to the end of your seam. Take an extra couple of stitches, and then slip your next pair under your presser foot and keep sewing. Repeat until you've assembled all your units, then clip them apart, press, and move on to the next set of units. ✳

ASSEMBLING THE QUILT TOP

1. Paying careful attention to the orientation of the blocks, lay out the blocks, light gray 10½" × 20½" rectangles, and light gray 10½" squares in four rows. Join the pieces in each row. Press. Join the rows. Press. Repeat to make a total of four quadrants measuring 40½" square.

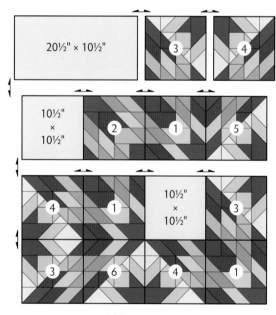

Make 4 quarters,
40½" × 40½".

2. Refer to the quilt assembly diagram above right to arrange the quadrants in two rows of two quadrants each as shown, rotating each quadrant a quarter turn to form the design. Join the pieces in each row. Press. Join the rows. Press. The quilt top should measure 80½" square.

Quilt assembly

3. Sew the light gray 5½" × 42" strips together end to end to make one long strip. From the pieced strip, cut two 5½" × 80½" strips. Sew these strips to the sides of the quilt top. Press the seam allowances toward the strips. From the remainder of the pieced strip, cut two 5½" × 90½" strips. Sew these strips to the top and bottom of the quilt top. Press the seam allowances toward the strips. The quilt top should measure 90½" square.

FINISHING

1. Layer the quilt top, batting, and backing. Baste the layers together.

2. Hand or machine quilt as desired. The quilt shown is machine quilted with an allover swirl and feather design.

3. Use the navy textural print 2½"-wide strips to make the binding; attach the binding to the quilt.

Alternate Layout

It's always fun to take a single block from a complex quilt such as Dream Catcher and turn it into a "one-block wonder" kind of project. For example, if you make a quilt using only block 1 from this pattern, you end up with another amazing star quilt! Make 64 blocks using the light gray textural print for pieces A and D. Lay out the blocks in eight rows of eight blocks each, rotating the blocks to form the pattern. ✳

Snow Kissed

Feel like a magician as you use two different blocks, along with some clever stitch-and-flip sashing units, to create the illusion of interwoven stars. Because these blocks are so intricate, use low-volume prints (or prints that read almost like a solid) in white and gray to really allow the blocks to become the focal point of the quilt. Keep the gradation in the fabrics subtle and it will appear that moonlight is reflecting off freshly fallen snow.

SKILL LEVEL:

FINISHED QUILT SIZE: 96½" × 96½"
FINISHED BLOCK SIZE: 12" × 12"

MATERIALS

Yardage is based on 42"-wide fabric.

 2⅛ yards of white-on-white constellation print for blocks and sashing

 ⅝ yard of white-on-medium-gray low-volume print for Snowflake blocks and sashing

 8⅓ yards of sapphire blue textural print for background

 1 yard of medium gray mottled print for blocks and sashing

 1⅛ yards of light gray low-volume print for Star blocks and sashing

 1 yard of light gray textural print for Star blocks and sashing

 ⅔ yard of very light gray-on-white print for sashing

⅔ yard of gray-on-white print for sashing

⅞ yard of dark gray solid for binding

8¾ yards of fabric for backing

105" × 105" square of batting

CUTTING

All measurements include ¼"-wide seam allowances. Label your pieces as you cut. During block assembly, each piece will be referred to by the letter following the dimensions of the piece.

From the white-on-white constellation print, cut:
8 strips, 3½" × 42"; crosscut into 152 rectangles, 2" × 3½" (A)
20 strips, 2" × 42"; crosscut into 396 squares, 2" × 2" (D)

From the white-on-medium-gray low-volume print, cut:
2 strips, 3½" × 42"; crosscut into 13 squares, 3½" × 3½" (G)
6 strips, 2" × 42"; crosscut into 104 squares, 2" × 2" (B)

Continued on page 56

Continued from page 55

From the sapphire blue textural print, cut:

2 strips, 12½" × 42"; crosscut into 20 rectangles,
    3½" × 12½" (T)

9 strips, 6½" × 42"; crosscut into:
    20 squares, 6½" × 6½"
    52 rectangles, 3½" × 6½" (R)

9 strips, 5" × 42"; crosscut into 96 rectangles,
    3½" × 5" (S)

27 strips, 3½" × 42"; crosscut into:
    152 squares, 3½" × 3½" (C)
    264 rectangles, 2" × 3½" (O)

2 strips, 2⅜" × 42"; crosscut into 24 squares,
    2⅜" × 2⅜" (M)

22 strips, 2" × 42"; crosscut into 424 squares,
    2" × 2" (F)

From the medium gray mottled print, cut:

6 strips, 3½" × 42"; crosscut into:
    12 squares, 3½" × 3½" (P)
    104 rectangles, 2" × 3½" (E)

5 strips, 2" × 42"; crosscut into 96 squares, 2" × 2" (I)

From the light gray low-volume print, cut:

5 strips, 3½" × 42"; crosscut into 96 rectangles,
    2" × 3½" (H)

8 strips, 2" × 42"; crosscut into 144 squares,
    2" × 2" (K)

From the light gray textural print, cut:

5 strips, 3½" × 42"; crosscut into 96 rectangles,
    2" × 3½" (J)

2 strips, 2⅜" × 42"; crosscut into 24 squares,
    2⅜" × 2⅜" (N)

5 strips, 2" × 42"; crosscut into 96 squares, 2" × 2" (L)

From the very light gray-on-white print, cut:

6 strips, 3½" × 42"; crosscut into 104 rectangles,
    2" × 3½" (Q)

From the gray-on-white print, cut:

2 strips, 3½" × 42"; crosscut into 16 squares,
    3½" × 3½" (V)

7 strips, 2" × 42"; crosscut into 128 squares,
    2" × 2" (U)

From the dark gray solid, cut:

10 strips, 2½" × 42"

MAKING THE SNOWFLAKE BLOCKS

Use a ¼" seam allowance. Press the seam allowances as indicated by the arrows in the illustrations. Measurements given for assembled pieces include seam allowances.

1. Make 52 flying-geese units (see page 10) using A rectangles and B squares. Press. Each unit should measure 2" × 3½".

Make 52 units,
2" × 3½".

2. Make 52 house units (see page 10) using C and D squares. Press. Each unit should measure 3½" square.

Make 52 house units,
3½" × 3½".

3. Join one unit each from steps 1 and 2 to make a Flying Geese variation block. Press. Repeat to make a total of 52 blocks measuring 3½" × 5".

Make 52 Flying Geese variation blocks,
3½" × 5".

4. Using E rectangles and D and F squares, make 52 right-leaning units (see page 12). Press. Each unit should measure 2" × 3½".

Make 52 units,
2" × 3½".

By Shelley Cavanna; quilted by Cara Cansler

5. Using A and E rectangles and F squares, make 52 left-leaning units (see page 10). Press. Each unit should measure 2" × 5".

Make 52 units,
2" × 5".

6. Join one unit each from steps 4 and 5 with a C square to make a Half-Log-Cabin block. Press and repeat to make a total of 52 blocks measuring 5" square.

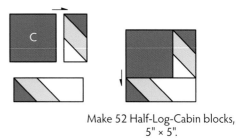

Make 52 Half-Log-Cabin blocks,
5" × 5".

7. Lay out the Flying Geese blocks, the Half-Log-Cabin blocks, and a G square in three horizontal rows as shown. Join the pieces in each row. Press. Join the rows. Press. Repeat to make a total of 13 Snowflake blocks measuring 12½" square.

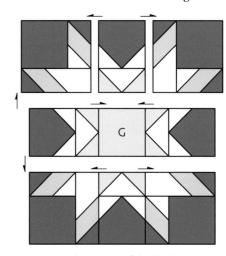

Make 13 Snowflake blocks,
12½" × 12½".

MAKING THE STAR BLOCKS

1. Make 48 sets of three flying-geese units using A, H, and J rectangles and I, K, and L squares. Press. Each unit should measure 2" × 3½".

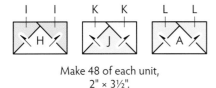

Make 48 of each unit,
2" × 3½".

2. Join one set of flying-geese units as shown to make a Flying Geese block. Press. Repeat to make a total of 48 blocks measuring 3½" × 5".

Make 48 Flying Geese blocks,
3½" × 5".

3. Using M and N squares, make 48 half-square-triangle units (see page 10). Press. Each unit should measure 2" square.

Make 48 units,
2" × 2".

4. Sew a K square to the left end of an O rectangle to make a stitch-and-flip corner (see page 9). Press and repeat to make a total of 48 units measuring 2" × 3½".

Make 48 units,
2" × 3½".

5. Sew an F square to the left end of a J rectangle to make a stitch-and-flip corner. Press and repeat to make a total of 48 units measuring 2" × 3½".

Make 48 units,
2" × 3½".

6. Make 48 left-leaning units using O and H rectangles. Press. Each unit should measure 2" × 5".

Make 48 units,
2" × 5".

7. Join one unit each from steps 3–6 with a D square to make a Half-Log-Cabin block. Repeat to make a total of 48 blocks measuring 5" square.

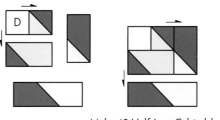

Make 48 Half-Log-Cabin blocks,
5" × 5".

8. Lay out the Flying Geese blocks, Half-Log-Cabin blocks, and a P square in three horizontal rows as shown. Join the pieces in each row. Join the rows. Make a total of 12 blocks measuring 12½" square.

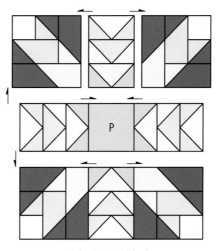

Make 12 Star blocks,
12½" × 12½".

MAKING THE SASHING UNITS

1. Make 52 right-leaning units and 52 left-leaning units using Q rectangles and F squares. Each unit should measure 2" × 3½".

Make 52 of each unit,
2" × 3½".

2. Join right- and left-leaning units from step 1 with O and R rectangles as shown to make a Snowflake block sashing unit; press. Repeat to make a total of 52 units measuring 3½" × 12½".

Make 52 Snowflake block sashing units,
3½" × 12½".

3. Make 48 house units using C and D squares. Press. Each unit should measure 3½" square.

Make 48 house units,
3½" × 3½".

4. Join S rectangles to the left and right sides of a house unit from step 3; press. Repeat to make a total of 48 units measuring 3½" × 12½".

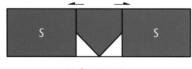

Make 48 units,
3½" × 12½".

5. Using D squares, make stitch-and-flip corners on the lower corners of each unit from step 4 to complete the Star block sashing units; press. Each unit should measure 3½" × 12½".

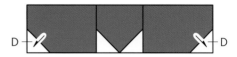

Make 48 Star block sashing units,
3½" × 12½".

6. Join a Snowflake block sashing unit and a Star block sashing unit as shown to make an inner sashing unit, paying careful attention to the orientation of the units. Press. Repeat to make a total of 40 inner sashing units measuring 6½" × 12½".

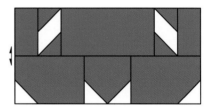

Make 40 inner sashing units,
6½" × 12½".

7. Join a T rectangle to the top edge of each of the remaining 12 Snowflake block sashing units and eight Star block sashing units to make the border units. Press. Each unit should measure 6½" × 12½".

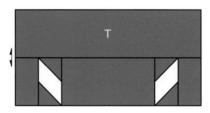

Make 12 Snowflake block border units,
6½" × 12½".

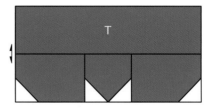

Make 8 Starblock border units,
6½" × 12½".

8. Make 64 flying-geese units using O rectangles and U squares; each unit should measure 2" × 3½".

Make 64 units,
2" × 3½".

9. Lay out four flying-geese units, four F squares, and a V square in three horizontal rows as shown. Join the pieces in each row. Press. Join the rows. Press. Repeat to make a total of 16 sashing cornerstone squares measuring 6½" square.

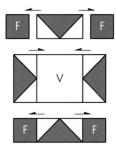 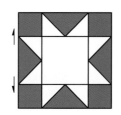

Make 16 cornerstone squares,
6½" × 6½".

ASSEMBLING THE QUILT TOP

Refer to the quilt assembly diagram below to lay out the Snowflake and Star blocks, the sashing units and squares, and the blue 6½" squares in 11 horizontal rows, being careful that all of the sashing units are rotated correctly. Join the pieces in each row. Press. Join the rows. Press. The quilt top should measure 96½" square.

FINISHING

1. Layer the quilt top, batting, and backing. Baste the layers together.

2. Hand or machine quilt as desired. The quilt shown is machine quilted with an allover design of five-petal flowers.

3. Use the dark gray 2½"-wide strips to make the binding; attach the binding to the quilt.

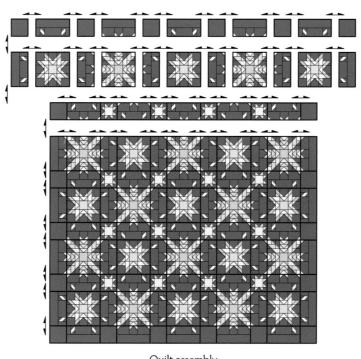

Quilt assembly

Crystalline

Prepare to be amazed—the stars in Crystalline aren't constructed like you might think! Using a combination of Half-Log-Cabin and Star Tip blocks, along with pieced sashing units and negative space, you'll create the illusion of stars that seem to float in the air.

SKILL LEVEL:

FINISHED QUILT SIZE: 72½" × 72½"

FINISHED BLOCK SIZES:

- Star block: 12" × 12"
- Star Tip block: 6" × 6"

MATERIALS

Yardage is based on 42"-wide fabric.

 ⅝ yard of small-scale red print for Star blocks

 4¼ yards of mint textural print for background and border

 ½ yard of small-scale cream print for Star blocks

 ¾ yard of cream textural print for Star Tip blocks and sashing cornerstone squares

 ¾ yard of red textural print for Star Tip blocks and sashing cornerstone squares

 ¾ yard of medium-scale taupe print for Star Tip blocks and sashing cornerstone squares

 ⅔ yard of medium-scale cream print for Star Tip blocks and sashing cornerstone squares

⅔ yard of red plaid for binding

4½ yards of fabric for backing

79" × 79" square of batting

CUTTING

All measurements include ¼"-wide seam allowances. Label your pieces as you cut. During block assembly, each piece will be referred to by the letter following the dimensions of the piece.

From the small-scale red print, cut:
3 strips, 3½" × 42"; crosscut into 48 rectangles, 2" × 3½" (A)
3 strips, 2" × 42"; crosscut into 48 squares, 2" × 2" (D)

From the mint textural print, cut:
2 strips, 12½" × 42"; crosscut into 4 squares, 12½" × 12½"
2 strips, 6½" × 42"; crosscut into 12 squares, 6½" × 6½" (R)
6 strips, 5" × 42"; crosscut into 48 squares, 5" × 5" (E)
17 strips, 3½" × 42"; crosscut *9 of the strips* into 168 rectangles, 2" × 3½" (B)
4 strips, 2" × 42"; crosscut into 72 squares, 2" × 2" (L)

From the small-scale cream print, cut:
3 strips, 5" × 42"; crosscut into 48 rectangles, 2" × 5" (C)

Continued on page 64

Continued from page 63

From the cream textural print, cut:

2 strips, 5" × 42"; crosscut into 36 rectangles,
   2" × 5" (N)

2 strips, 3½" × 42"; crosscut into 36 rectangles,
   2" × 3½" (Q)

2 strips, 2⅜" × 42"; crosscut into 18 squares,
   2⅜" × 2⅜" (F)

From the medium-scale taupe print, cut:

2 strips, 5" × 42"; crosscut into 36 rectangles,
   2" × 5" (M)

2 strips, 3½" × 42"; crosscut into 36 rectangles,
   2" × 3½" (K)

2 strips, 2⅜" × 42"; crosscut into 18 squares,
   2⅜" × 2⅜" (G)

From the medium-scale cream print, cut:

2 strips, 5" × 42"; crosscut into 36 rectangles,
   2" × 5" (P)

2 strips, 3½" × 42"; crosscut into 36 rectangles,
   2" × 3½" (H)

2 strips, 2" × 42"; crosscut into 36 squares, 2" × 2" (O)

From the red textural print, cut:

2 strips, 5" × 42"; crosscut into 36 rectangles,
   2" × 5" (J)

6 strips, 2" × 42"; crosscut into 108 squares, 2" × 2" (I)

From the red plaid, cut:

8 strips, 2½" × 42"

MAKING THE STAR BLOCKS

Use a ¼" seam allowance. Press the seam allowances as indicated by the arrows in the illustrations. Measurements given for assembled pieces include seam allowances.

1. Using A and B rectangles, make 48 right-leaning units (page 12). Press. Each should measure 2" × 5".

Make 48 units,
2" × 5".

2. Using B and C rectangles and D squares, make 48 left-leaning units (see page 10). Press. Each unit should measure 2" × 6½".

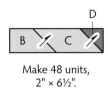

Make 48 units,
2" × 6½".

3. Join one unit each from steps 1 and 2 with an E square to make a Half-Log-Cabin block. Press and repeat to make a total of 48 blocks measuring 6½" square.

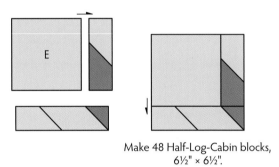

Make 48 Half-Log-Cabin blocks,
6½" × 6½".

4. Lay out four Half-Log-Cabin blocks in two horizontal rows of two blocks each as shown. Press. Repeat to make a total of 12 Star blocks measuring 12½" square.

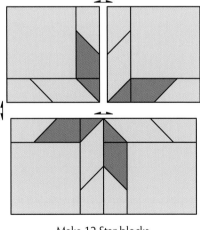

Make 12 Star blocks,
12½" × 12½".

By Shelley Cavanna; quilted by Darby Myers

MAKING THE SASHING UNITS

1. Using F and G squares, make 36 half-square-triangle units (see page 10). Press. Each unit should measure 2" square.

Make 36 units,
2" × 2".

2. Sew an I square to the right end of an H rectangle to make a stitch-and-flip corner (see page 9). Press and repeat to make a total of 36 units measuring 2" × 3½".

Make 36 units,
2" × 3½".

3. Arrange one unit each from steps 1 and 2 with an I square in two horizontal rows. Sew the pieces in the top row together. Press. Sew the unit from step 2 to the bottom of the joined pieces to make a half-log-cabin unit. Press. Repeat to make a total of 36 units measuring 3½" square.

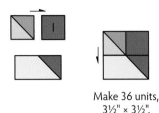

Make 36 units,
3½" × 3½".

4. Arrange four half-log-cabin units in two horizontal rows of two units each as shown. Join the units in each row. Press. Join the rows. Press. Repeat to make a total of nine sashing cornerstone squares measuring 6½" square.

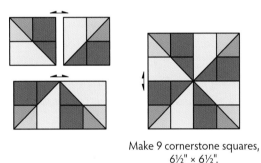

Make 9 cornerstone squares,
6½" × 6½".

5. Make 36 sets of two right-leaning units using B, J, K, and M rectangles and I and L squares. Press. Each unit should measure 2" × 6½".

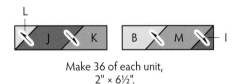

Make 36 of each unit,
2" × 6½".

6. Make 36 sets of two left-leaning units using B, N, P, and Q rectangles and L and O squares. Press. Each unit should measure 2" × 6½".

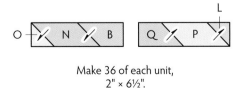

Make 36 of each unit,
2" × 6½".

7. Join one set each from steps 5 and 6 as shown to make a Star Tip block. Press. Repeat to make a total of 36 blocks measuring 6½" square.

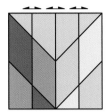

Make 36 Star Tip blocks,
6½" × 6½".

8. Sew an R square to the top of a Star Tip block to make a single star-tip unit. Press. Repeat to make a total of 12 units measuring 6½" × 12½".

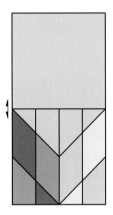

Make 12 single star-tip units,
6½" × 12½".

9. Join two Star Tip blocks as shown to make a double star tip unit. Press. Repeat to make a total of 12 units measuring 6½" × 12½".

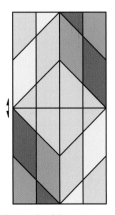

Make 12 double star-tip units,
6½" × 12½".

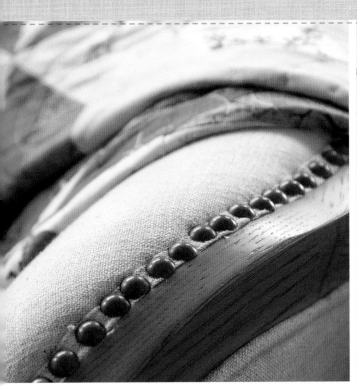

ASSEMBLING THE QUILT TOP

1. Refer to the quilt assembly diagram below to lay out the Star blocks, sashing units, and mint 12½" squares in seven horizontal rows. Join the pieces in each row. Press. Join the rows to make the quilt center. Press. The quilt top should measure 66½" square.

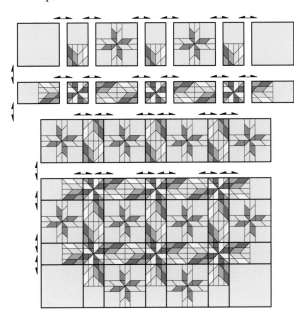

Quilt-center assembly

2. Join two mint 3½" × 42" strips end to end. Press the seam allowances open. Repeat with the remaining mint 3½" × 42" strips to make a total of four pieced strips. From the pieced strips, cut two 3½" × 66½" strips and sew them to the sides of the quilt top. Press the seam allowances toward the strips. Cut two 3½" × 72½" strips from the remaining two pieced strips. Sew these strips to the top and bottom edges of the quilt top. Press the seam allowances toward the strips. The quilt top should measure 72½" square.

FINISHING

1. Layer the quilt top, batting, and backing. Baste the layers together.

2. Hand or machine quilt as desired. The quilt shown is quilted using an allover swirl design with snowflakes sprinkled throughout.

3. Use the red plaid 2½"-wide strips to make the binding; attach the binding to the quilt.

Wavelength

Normally a quilt this complex would require lots of mirror-image templates or paper-pieced units, but using the stitch-and-flip method with rectangles of different lengths allows you to achieve the same look without all the fuss. And, because of all the spacing between blocks, there are very few points to line up—bonus!

SKILL LEVEL: ✳ ✳ ✳

FINISHED QUILT SIZE: 108½" × 108½"

FINISHED BLOCK SIZES:

- Block 1: 18" × 18"
- Block 2: 28" × 28"
- Blocks 3 and 4: 18" × 28"
- Block 5: 8" × 18"
- Block 6: 8" × 28"

MATERIALS

Yardage is based on 42"-wide fabric.

 1⅛ yards of pear green print for blocks

 ⅞ yard of small-scale navy print for blocks

 11½ yards of light gray textural print for background and border

 ⅞ yard of light teal print for blocks

 1¾ yards of navy textural print for blocks and binding

 1⅛ yards of golden yellow print for blocks

 ⅞ yard of raspberry pink textural print for blocks

 ⅞ yard of dark teal print for blocks

 ⅔ yard of small-scale raspberry pink print for blocks

 ⅞ yard of coral print for blocks

9¾ yards of fabric for backing

117" × 117" square of batting

CUTTING

All measurements include ¼"-wide seam allowances. Label your pieces as you cut. During block assembly, each piece will be referred to by the letter following the dimensions of the piece.

From the pear green print, cut:
4 strips, 8½" × 42"; crosscut into:
    28 rectangles, 4½" × 8½" (G)
    4 squares, 4½" × 4½" (B)

From the small-scale navy print, cut:
6 strips, 4½" × 42"; crosscut into:
    12 rectangles, 4½" × 8½" (T)
    20 squares, 4½" × 4½" (C)

Continued on page 70

Continued from page 69

From the light gray textural print, cut:

25 strips, 6½" × 42"; crosscut into:

    8 rectangles, 6½" × 18½" (HH)

    168 rectangles, 4½" × 6½" (A)

    2 squares, 4⅞" × 4⅞" (Q)

25 strips, 4½" × 42"; crosscut *14 of the strips* into:

    32 rectangles, 4½" × 10½" (R)

    32 squares, 4½" × 4½" (S)

40 strips, 2½" × 42"; crosscut into:

    4 strips, 2½" × 28½" (FF)

    4 strips, 2½" × 26½" (EE)

    28 strips, 2½" × 22½" (DD)

    4 strips, 2½" × 20½" (CC)

    4 strips, 2½" × 18½" (O)

    8 strips, 2½" × 16½" (N)

    4 strips, 2½" × 14½" (V)

    4 strips, 2½" × 12½" (M)

    8 strips, 2½" × 10½" (L)

    4 rectangles, 2½" × 8½" (U)

    4 rectangles, 2½" × 6½" (K)

    4 rectangles, 2½" × 4½" (J)

From the light teal print, cut:

3 strips, 8½" × 42"; crosscut into:

    20 rectangles, 4½" × 8½" (D)

    2 squares, 4⅞" × 4⅞" (P)

From the navy textural print, cut:

3 strips, 8½" × 42"; crosscut into:

    20 rectangles, 4½" × 8½" (H)

    4 squares, 4½" × 4½" (E)

12 strips, 2½" × 42"

From the golden yellow print, cut:

3 strips, 8½" × 42"; crosscut into 24 rectangles,

    4½" × 8½" (X)

2 strips, 4½" × 42"; crosscut into 16 squares,

    4½" × 4½" (F)

From the raspberry pink textural print, cut:

6 strips, 4½" × 42"; crosscut into:

    8 rectangles, 4½" × 8½" (GG)

    28 squares, 4½" × 4½" (I)

From the dark teal print, cut:

3 strips, 8½" × 42"; crosscut into:

    20 rectangles, 4½" × 8½" (AA)

    4 squares, 4½" × 4½" (W)

From the small-scale raspberry pink print, cut:

2 strips, 8½" × 42"; crosscut into:

    1 square, 8½" × 8½" (JJ)

    16 rectangles, 4½" × 8½" (Y)

1 strip, 4½" × 42"; crosscut into 8 squares,

    4½" × 4½" (II)

From the coral print, cut:

3 strips, 8½" × 42"; crosscut into:

    20 rectangles, 4½" × 8½" (BB)

    4 squares, 4½" × 4½" (Z)

Make Two Quilts at Once!

The leftover triangle trimmings are perfect for a bonus half-square-triangle project. Because all the units you're sewing are already matched in print/background pairs, take the time to stitch a second seam ½" from the first on the side of the seam that you'll be trimming away. You can either draw a second line or just eyeball the distance. Then, when you cut the units apart, you'll have a block for this quilt plus a bonus half-square-triangle block! If you do this with each stitch-and-flip block, you'll end up with almost 400 blocks to use in my favorite half-square-triangle project on page 78. ✳

MAKING BLOCK 1

Use a ¼" seam allowance. Press the seam allowances as indicated by the arrows in the illustrations. Measurements given for assembled pieces include seam allowances.

1. Sew B and C squares to an A rectangle to make a right-leaning unit (see page 12). Press. Repeat to make a total of four units measuring 4½" × 6½".

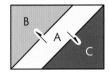

Make 4 units,
4½" × 6½".

2. Using A and D rectangles and E and F squares, make four right-leaning units. Press. Each unit should measure 4½" × 12½".

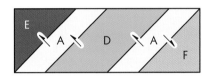

Make 4 units,
4½" × 12½".

3. Using A and G rectangles and C squares, make four left-leaning units (see page 10). Press. Each unit should measure 4½" × 10½".

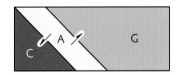

Make 4 units,
4½" × 10½".

4. Using A, D, and H rectangles and F squares, make four left-leaning units. Press. Each unit should measure 4½" × 16½".

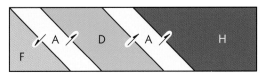

Make 4 units,
4½" × 16½".

5. Join one unit each from steps 1–4 with an I square and J–O rectangles to make a half-log-cabin unit. Press after adding each piece. Repeat to make a total of four blocks measuring 18½" square.

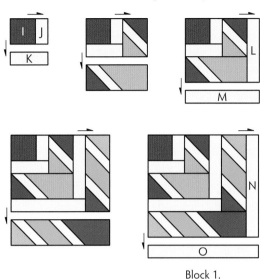

Block 1.
Make 4 blocks,
18½" × 18½".

MAKING BLOCK 2

1. Using P and Q squares, make four half-square-triangle units (see page 10). Press. Each unit should measure 4½" square.

Make 4 units,
4½" × 4½".

2. Sew a C square to the left end of an R rectangle to make a stitch-and-flip corner (see page 9). Press. Repeat to make a total of four units measuring 4½" × 10½".

Make 4 units,
4½" × 10½".

3. Sew S squares to the left ends of D rectangles to make four stitch-and-flip corner units measuring 4½" × 8½".

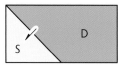

Make 4 units,
4½" × 8½".

4. Using R and T rectangles, make four left-leaning units. Press. Each unit should measure 4½" × 14½".

Make 4 units, 4½" × 14½".

5. Join one unit each from steps 1–4 with an S square and L, N, U, and V rectangles to make a half-log-cabin unit. Press after each piece. Make four half-log-cabin units measuring 16½" square.

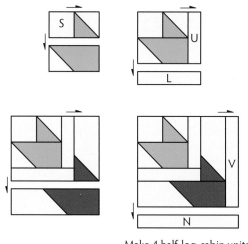

Make 4 half-log-cabin units,
16½" × 16½".

6. Using A, G, and X rectangles and S and W squares, make four right-leaning units. Press. Each unit should measure 4½" × 16½".

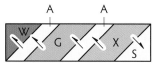

Make 4 units, 4½" × 16½".

7. Using A, H, R, and GG rectangles and Z squares, make four right-leaning units. Press. Each unit should measure 4½" × 22½".

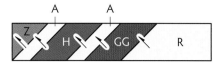

Make 4 units, 4½" × 22½".

8. Using A, G, X, and AA rectangles and S squares, make four left-leaning units. Each unit should measure 4½" × 20½".

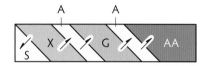

Make 4 units, 4½" × 20½".

9. Using A, H, R, BB, and GG rectangles, make four left-leaning units. Each unit should measure 4½" × 26½".

Make 4 units, 4½" × 26½".

10. Join one half-log-cabin unit from step 5 with one unit each from steps 6–9 and CC–FF rectangles to make block 2. Press after adding each piece. Repeat to make a total of four blocks measuring 28½" square.

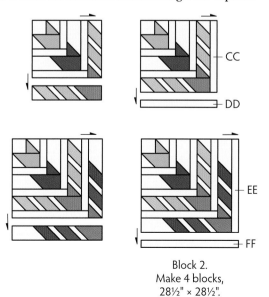

Block 2.
Make 4 blocks,
28½" × 28½".

MAKING BLOCK 3

1. Using A, G, R, X, Y, AA, and BB rectangles and C, F, I, and S squares, make four sets of right-leaning units. Press. Each unit should measure 4½" × 22½".

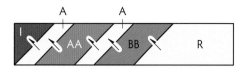

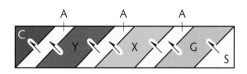

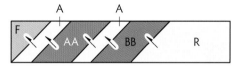

Make 4 of each unit,
4½" × 22½".

2. Paying careful attention to the position of each unit, join one of each of the step 1 units along with DD rectangles as shown. Press. Join an HH rectangle to the top of the unit. Press. Repeat to make a total of four blocks measuring 18½" × 28½".

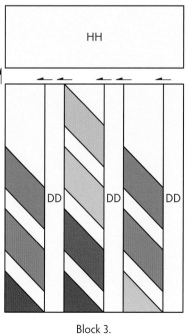

Block 3.
Make 4 blocks,
18½" × 28½".

MAKING BLOCK 4

1. Using A, G, R, X, Y, AA, and BB rectangles and I, C, F, and S squares, make four sets of left-leaning units. Press. Each unit should measure 4½" × 22½".

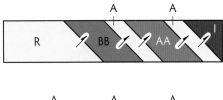

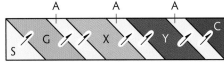

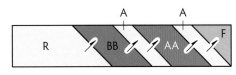

Make 4 of each unit,
4½" × 22½".

2. Paying careful attention to the position of each unit, join one of each of the step 1 units, along with DD rectangles. Press. Join an HH rectangle to the top of the unit. Press. Repeat to make a total of four blocks measuring 18½" × 28½".

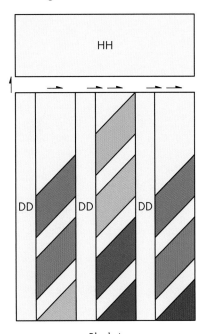

Block 4.
Make 4 blocks,
18½" × 28½".

MAKING BLOCK 5

1. Using A, G, and X rectangles and I and II squares, make four sets of right- and left-leaning units. Press. Each unit should measure 4½" × 18½".

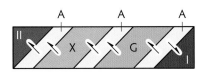

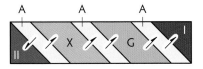

Make 4 of each unit,
4½" × 18½".

2. Paying careful attention to the orientation of the units, join one of each step 1 unit to make block 5. Press. Repeat to make a total of four blocks measuring 8½" × 18½".

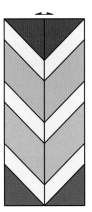

Block 5.
Make 4 blocks,
8½" × 18½".

MAKING BLOCK 6

1. Using A, D, H, T, and Y rectangles and S and I squares, make four sets of right- and left-leaning units. Press. Each unit should measure 4½" × 28½".

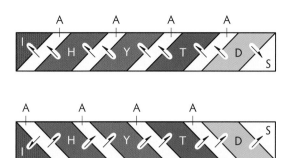

Make 4 of each unit,
4½" × 28½".

2. Paying careful attention to the orientation of the units, join one of each step 1 unit to make block 6. Press. Repeat to make a total of four blocks measuring 8½" × 28½".

Block 6.
Make 4 blocks,
8½" × 28½".

By Shelley Cavanna; quilted by Darby Myers

ASSEMBLING THE QUILT TOP

1. Referring to the quilt-center assembly diagram and paying careful attention to the orientation of the blocks, arrange blocks 1–6 and the JJ square in five horizontal rows. Join the pieces in each row. Press. Join the rows. Press. The quilt center should measure 100½" square.

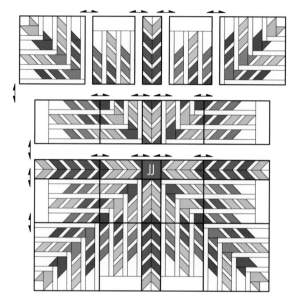

Quilt-center assembly

2. Join five light gray textural 4½" × 42" strips end to end to make one long strip. Press the seam allowances open. From the pieced strip, cut two strips, 4½" × 100½". Sew the strips to the sides of the quilt top. Press the seam allowances toward the strips. Join three light gray textural 4½" × 42" strips in the same manner. Repeat with the remaining three strips to make a total of two pieced strips. From each pieced strip, cut one strip, 4½" × 108½". Sew these strips to the top and bottom edges of the quilt top. Press the seam allowances toward the strips. The quilt top should measure 108½" square.

FINISHING

1. Layer the quilt top, batting, and backing. Baste the layers together.

2. Hand or machine quilt as desired. The quilt shown is machine quilted with a geometric design.

3. Use the navy textural print 2½"-wide strips to make the binding; attach the binding to the quilt.

Alternate Layout

To make a lap-sized version of Wavelength, make four of block 2 *but do not attach the EE and FF rectangles.* Join the blocks in two rows of two blocks, along with 2"-wide (finished) sashing and borders for a quilt that finishes at 58½" square. ✳

Use Your Leftover Half-Square Triangles

Did you stitch all the bonus half-square triangles while piecing Wavelength on page 69? If so, you're halfway to completing this 63½" square quilt, which will use up a good deal of them! Here's what you need.

Make 24 units. Make 27 units. Make 32 units.

Make 36 units. Make 38 units. Make 39 units.

Make 40 units. Make 42 units. Make 51 units.

MATERIALS

Yardage is based on 42"-wide fabric.

328 half-square-triangle units from Wavelength

1⅛ yards of light gray textural print for background

⅝ yard of dark gray print for binding

4 yards of fabric for backing

70" × 70" square of batting

CUTTING

From the light gray textural print, cut:
10 strips, 3½" × 42"; crosscut into:
> 2 strips, 3½" × 39½" (A)
> 2 strips, 3½" × 33½" (B)
> 2 strips, 3½" × 27½" (C)
> 2 rectangles, 3½" × 9½" (D)
> 2 strips, 3½" × 23" (E)
> 2 strips, 3½" × 21½" (F)
> 2 strips, 3½" × 15½" (G)
> 2 squares, 3½" × 3½" (H)

From the dark gray print, cut:
7 strips, 2½" × 42"

ASSEMBLING AND FINISHING THE QUILT

1. Press the seam allowances on all of the half-square-triangle units toward the background print. Square up each unit to 3½" square.

2. Paying careful attention to the rotation of the units, lay out all the trimmed half-square-triangle units and the light gray pieces as shown. Just place the colors randomly! When you're satisfied with the arrangement, join the pieces in each row. Press. Join the rows. Press. The quilt top should measure 63½" square.

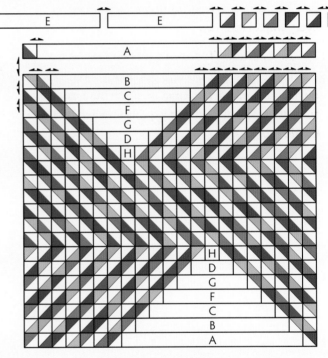

Quilt assembly

3. Layer the quilt top, batting, and backing. Baste the layers together. Hand or machine quilt as desired. Use the dark gray 2½"-wide strips to make the binding; attach the binding to the quilt.

Acknowledgments

It takes a tribe to write a book, and mere words will never be enough to express all the gratitude I feel right now!

✳ To my amazing husband, Rob, and our lads, Aiden and Jamie, for helping make all of this possible in so many ways. Thank you for your hugs, your patience, and for being my biggest cheerleaders every step of the way.

✳ To my granny, for helping me find my love of crafting at such an early age, and to my mom, who is not only my quilting partner in crime but has been so very helpful in getting my quilts finished and out the door on time!

✳ To my dad, for all of the Saturdays spent together at the dining-room table while I agonized over math homework. You were *completely* right about needing to use geometry in "real life."

✳ To Darby Myers of the Quilted Squid and Cara Cansler of Sew Colorado Quilting, for their superb and speedy long-arm quilting services.

✳ To my fabric family at Benartex and to Moda Fabrics and Andover Fabrics for providing the materials for this book.

✳ And finally, to my friendly publishing team, who so very kindly helped me navigate through the waters of writing my first book. I can't wait for our next project together!

Connect with Shelley

The sense of community is one of my favorite things about being a quilter. Here are a few ways to keep in touch and to hear about the happenings in my studio.

- Follow me on Instagram @**CorasQuilts**.

- Share your photos on Instagram using **#SpectacularStarsSimplified** and **#CorasQuilts** so that I can see your projects! Then check out these hashtags to see more projects from quilty friends.

- Subscribe to the monthly email newsletter at CorasQuilts.com/subscribe/ for information on recent blog posts, upcoming quilt-alongs, the occasional free pattern, Facebook community info, and loads of other goodies!

About the Author

Photo by Leann Thompson, Leann Marie Photography

Shelley Cavanna is a self-taught quilter, teacher, designer of textiles and quilts, and the owner of Cora's Quilts. She makes her home near Sacramento, California, with her husband and their two boys. She has a passion for modern, intricate, mosaic-inspired quilts and makes it her mission to turn these exquisite designs into approachable patterns for quilters of all styles and skill levels, living up to her design mantra, "Stunning quilts made simple." When she's not in the studio, Shelley loves hiking and exploring the Sierra Nevada Mountains or along the rugged Northern California coast with her boys. She is an avid reader (especially of historical fiction) and enjoys the occasional glass of red wine from Amador County. She loves yoga, despite being a little uncoordinated, and might even go so far as to classify herself as a halfway-decent knitter!